# Fire Safe Guide

**For multi-occupied, privately rented housing**

By Deborah Garvie and Roger Critchley

**Campaign for Bedsit Rights**

Shelter

Published by Shelter, 88 Old Street, London, EC1V 9HU
Registered Company 1038133
Registered Charity 263710

Design by Jon Checkley
Printed by Stanley L Hunt Printers Ltd

**Deborah Garvie** is a Policy Officer at Shelter's Campaign for Bedsit Rights.
**Roger Critchley** is an independent environmental health consultant and a member of the Health & Housing Group which specialises In providing expert reports on environmental health and housing problems. The Health and Housing Group can be contacted on 020 7233 7780.

## Acknowledgements
The authors would like to thank the following for their valuable technical and professional advice: Stephen Battersby, Russell Campbell, John Dalton, Rita Diaz, Richard Drew, Jon Gamble, Adair Lewis, Steve Lumb, Joe Marriott, Kevin Thompson, Suzanne Woodman. Thanks also to Nick Beacock and Jim Bennett for their support and assistance.

## Shelter
Shelter, the National Campaign for Homeless People, seeks to secure the provision of decent, secure and affordable housing as a basic human right. To achieve this, Shelter carries out a range of campaigning activities and provides practical advice services for badly housed and homeless people through a network of housing aid centres and projects throughout England and Scotland.
For further information about Shelter, please write to: Shelter, 88 Old Street, London EC1V 9HU. Telephone: 020 7505 2000. Fax: 020 7505 2169. E-mail: Shelterinfo@compuserve.com. Web site: www.shelter.org.uk

## Shelter's Campaign for Bedsit Rights
Shelter's Campaign for Bedsit Rights works to improve the housing conditions and rights of private tenants, particularly those living in houses in multiple occupation, through policy development, campaigning, rights information and research. One of our key campaigning aims is the introduction of a licensing scheme for all privately rented housing to ensure minimum standards of health, safety and management.

# Preface

Every year fire fighters are called to thousands of dwellings, many of them privately rented and multiply-occupied. They see, at first-hand, the devastating effects of fire on both people and property. They also know that the emotional and physical damage caused by even a minor fire can take months or years to rectify.

Much of this damage and disruption could so easily have been prevented. If fire hazards are identified and removed, and people have early warning of a fire so that it can be tackled in its earliest stages, much distress, time and money could be saved. If occupants are provided with a safe means of escape and are familiar with evacuation procedures, serious injury and loss of life can be avoided. It is sometimes the simplest measures that make the difference.

Fire does not discriminate. We believe that every person should be protected equally from the dangers of fire. Often, people who rent their homes privately are not aware that they have a legal right to accommodation which does not place them in needless danger. Multiply-occupied, multi-storey dwellings, such as bedsit houses and converted flats, are at the greatest risk of fire but often house the poorest and most vulnerable people. The law applies the strictest standards to these dwellings, but it is only if these standards are understood and applied that they will succeed in ensuring that people are adequately protected from death and injury.

We support Shelter's Campaign for Bedsit Rights in producing this valuable and unique guide. By making private tenants and their landlords aware of the practical action they should take, many more people, and their homes, will be safe from fire.

Fire Brigades Union
Fire Protection Association
National Fire Sprinkler Network
Residential Sprinkler Association

# How to use this guide

When you consider moving into privately rented accommodation, you are likely to look at the state of decoration, furnishing and repair of the property. The last thing that crosses many people's minds is whether the accommodation is safe from fire risks and whether they would be safe if a fire were to occur.

Yet this type of accommodation, especially in houses in multiple occupation, can contain lethal dangers. Government backed research[1] found that in the two year period 1994 to 1995, 126 people in England lost their lives as a result of fires in houses in multiple occupation. Many more were injured.

This Guide is written for anyone with an interest in eliminating these dangers and improving fire safety in this accommodation. It contains valuable practical advice for occupants and landlords. It is also intended to be useful to those advising them as well as to local authority officers and other professionals who specialise in enforcing fire safety standards.

**Chapter 1 *Understanding fire: page 5***
● explains the causes and effects of fire; outlines human behaviour when fires occur; and summarises the risks of death and injury by fire in multi-occupied houses.

**Chapter 2 *Identifying fire safety standards: page 16***
provides information to help you to decide which type of multi-occupied or private rented accommodation you live in or rent out, and gives an overview of the fire safety standards that apply to it.

**Chapter 3 *Fundamentals of fire safety: page 32***
● explains the main components of the standards outlined in Chapter 2. In particular, it contains detailed information on fire warning systems; means of escape; and fire fighting.

**Chapter 4 *What to do if standards are not met (1): page 64***
● provides detailed practical and legal advice for occupants and their advisers on how they can get the fire safety of their home improved if it does not meet the required standards.

**Chapter 5 *What to do if standards are not met (2): page 77***
● contains information for landlords about how they can get advice and support in meeting the fire safety standards for the accommodation they provide.

**Chapter 6 *What to do after a fire: page 81***
● contains information about what legal options occupiers have if a fire has occurred in their home.

---

 1. Department of the Environment, Transport and the Regions (1997) *Fire Risk in Houses in Multiple Occupation:* Research Report

# 1 Understanding fire

The most important thing about fire safety is understanding fire. If you are aware of:

● how fires start, develop and spread

● how fires affect people and their behaviour

● how the risks of injury or death from fire vary, depending on the building and its occupants.

then you will be more likely to appreciate the importance of fire safety measures. You will also be in a much better position to assess the dangers and risks in your particular circumstances.

**Having a realistic understanding of fire could save your life or the lives of others.**

## How do fires start?

The start of a fire is called ignition. This requires a source in the form of a flame, spark or heat. The majority of residential fires start accidentally from relatively ordinary sources of ignition: cookers, smokers' materials, candles, portable heaters, electrical appliances or electricity supplies.

**Figure 1: Accidental fires in all UK dwellings by source of ignition, 1997**

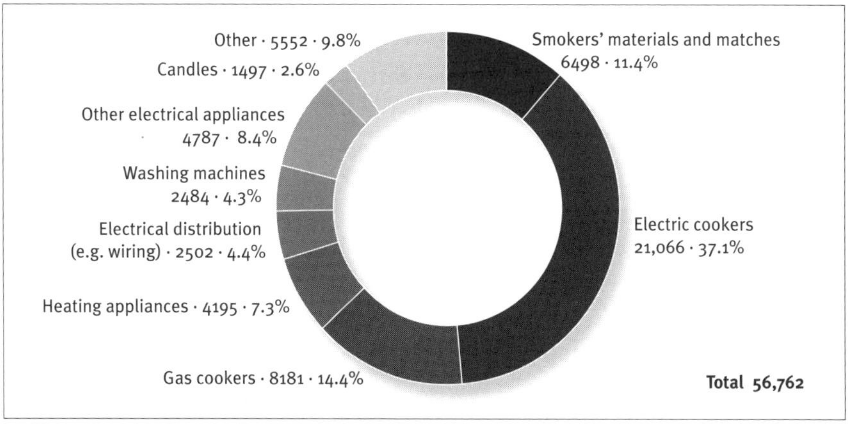

Other · 5552 · 9.8%
Candles · 1497 · 2.6%
Other electrical appliances · 4787 · 8.4%
Washing machines 2484 · 4.3%
Electrical distribution (e.g. wiring) · 2502 · 4.4%
Heating appliances · 4195 · 7.3%
Gas cookers · 8181 · 14.4%
Smokers' materials and matches 6498 · 11.4%
Electric cookers 21,066 · 37.1%
Total 56,762

(Source: Government Statistical Service (1998) Fire Statistics, United Kingdom, 1997)

The source of ignition is closely related to the cause of the fire. This is the defect, act or omission which led to ignition of the fire. For example, in most fires where the source of ignition was smokers' materials, the cause of the fire was the careless handling of these materials.

**Figure 2: Accidental fires in all UK dwellings by cause, 1997**

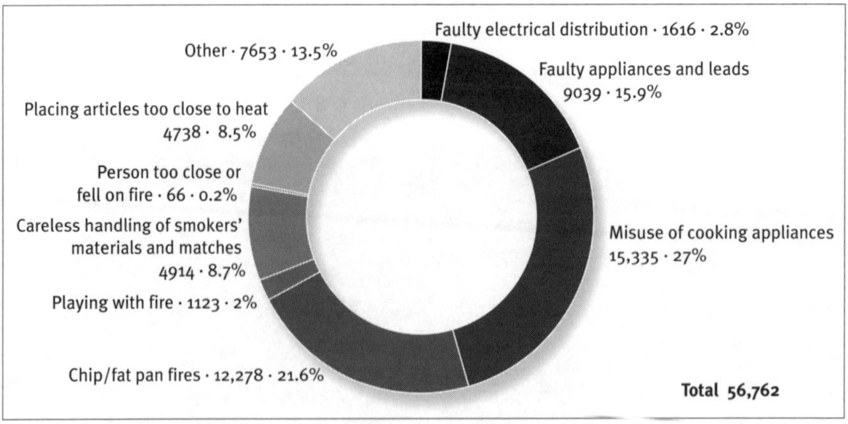

Faulty electrical distribution · 1616 · 2.8%

Other · 7653 · 13.5%

Faulty appliances and leads
9039 · 15.9%

Placing articles too close to heat
4738 · 8.5%

Person too close or
fell on fire · 66 · 0.2%

Careless handling of smokers'
materials and matches
4914 · 8.7%

Misuse of cooking appliances
15,335 · 27%

Playing with fire · 1123 · 2%

Chip/fat pan fires · 12,278 · 21.6%

Total 56,762

(Source: Government Statistical Service (1998) Fire Statistics, United Kingdom, 1997)

Although the majority of fires in dwellings begin accidentally, about 20% are started deliberately for malicious reasons.

## How do fires develop and spread?

After the fire has started, oxygen and fuel are needed to allow the fire to develop in what is called its growth period. During this period temperatures will remain relatively low and the chance of escaping safely is relatively high. This is why early warning systems (such as smoke detectors) are so important.

The length of the growth period largely depends on the size and contents of the room. The easier a material is to ignite and the greater the rate of heat it produces, the faster the fire will grow. The flames and heat from the original fire may start to ignite other nearby objects.

Heat from the fire will cause material in the room to give off gases and vapours. The resulting mixture of vapour and air may then itself ignite. Meanwhile the smoke from the original source will contain considerable heat. It will rise rapidly to the ceiling and spread out. It will heat up the surfaces and all the air in the room until a point is reached when anything capable of burning can easily be ignited. This is called flashover.

The fire will progress rapidly through flashover to the fully developed period. During this time all the combustibles (i.e. things that are capable of burning) in the room will start burning and the internal temperature will sharply increase. If the walls of the room do not form a tight joint with the ceiling, where the flames and hot gases are most severe, then the fire will soon penetrate into the space or room on the other side.

Even if the construction is fire resisting, the general buoyancy and expansion of fire gases can lead to them being driven to other parts of the building. Basically, the hot air is under pressure and will 'squirt' through any gap, crevice or crack. If the gases penetrate into an area like a liftwell, a vertical service duct or a stairwell (often described as a vertical shaft), they will rise rapidly. The fire gases will attack the top of this vertical shaft and spread into any openings. Even worse, if a substantial flow of air reaches the fire, say from an open door or window, then the vertical shaft will act like a chimney and the fire will grow very rapidly. This chimney effect is deadly, yet escape ladders leading to fire exits are sometimes positioned at the top of the 'chimney'. This is very dangerous.

If a house has been divided into separate units of accommodation (e.g. bedsits) or is shared by unrelated people, then the occupants will be less aware of what is happening in other parts of the building and may be less able to quickly alert others to a fire. In such houses, the speed at which the fire spreads to other parts of the building becomes even more important to the safety of the occupants. Figure 3 illustrates that in bedsit houses, shared houses and households with lodgers, over a third of fire deaths occur on floors above where the fire started. In the case of bedsits, there are as many deaths (44%) on floors above the origin of the fire as there are in the room where it started. This may well be because in such buildings there are fewer barriers to control the spread of fire, smoke and fumes (e.g. fire doors and lobbies) and protected escape routes than in hostels and purpose-built accommodation (e.g. halls of residence).

**Figure 3: Location of fatalities in relation to the fire in houses in multiple occupation**

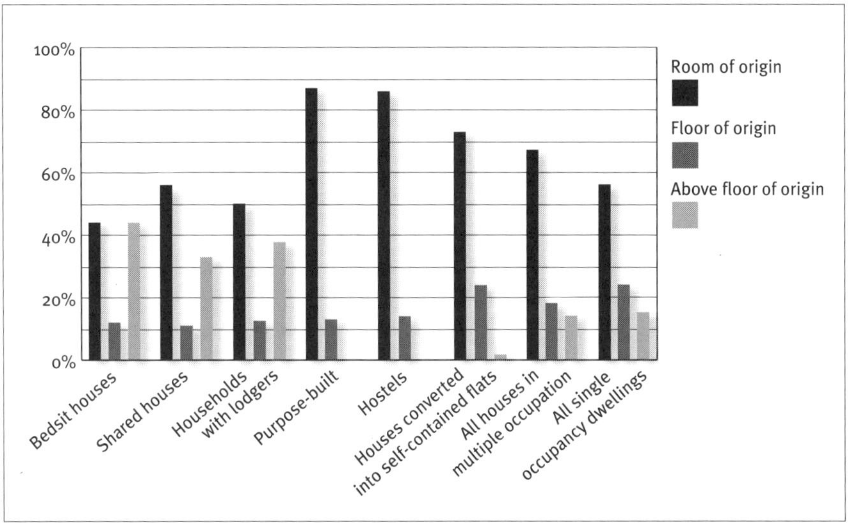

(Source: Department of the Environment, Transport & the Regions (1997) Fire Risk in Houses in Multiple Occupation: Research Report)

## The effects of fire on people

In the early stages of a fire the most dangerous effect will usually be from smoke and gases given off from burning. The most common poisonous gas is carbon monoxide.

In an enclosed space, the hot, smoke-laden gases will rise to form a layer which flows under the entire ceiling and then deepens. Once the smoke extends down to head height it will cause discomfort to the eyes and difficulty in breathing. This will interfere with people's efforts to find a way out.

Anyone who is prevented or delayed from escaping by dense smoke can suffer the poisonous effects of the products of combustion plus the asphyxiant (not being able to breathe) effect caused by the lack of oxygen. Half a per cent of carbon monoxide in the air causes rapid collapse, unconsciousness and death within a few minutes. Even lower concentrations of hydrogen cyanide from plastics (including polyurethane foam) can be immediately fatal or at least cause weakness, headaches and confusion.

**Figure 4: Fatal casualties in accidental dwelling fires, by cause of death, UK, 1997**

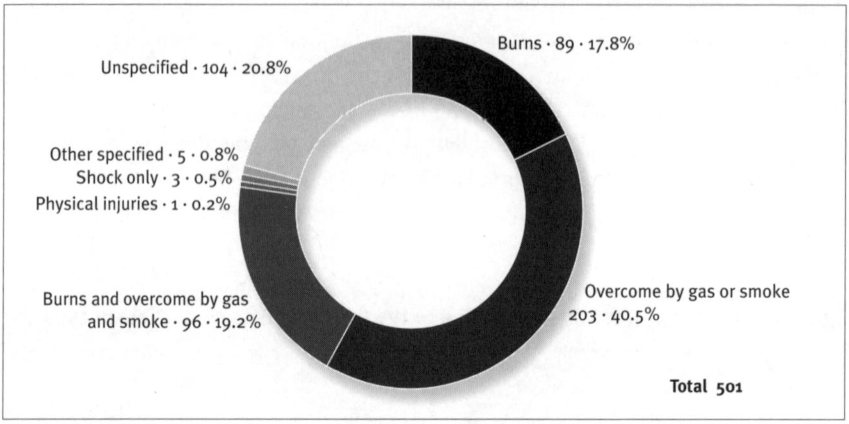

Burns · 89 · 17.8%

Unspecified · 104 · 20.8%

Other specified · 5 · 0.8%
Shock only · 3 · 0.5%
Physical injuries · 1 · 0.2%

Burns and overcome by gas
and smoke · 96 · 19.2%

Overcome by gas or smoke
203 · 40.5%

Total 501

(Source: Government Statistical Service (1998) Fire Statistics, United Kingdom, 1997)

Loss of life due to structural collapse is very rare. Figure 4 shows that over 40% of deaths in domestic fires were caused solely by the inhalation of fire gases and smoke, whilst a further 19% were caused by a combination of asphixiation and burns.

Research into single family houses shows that fires started in furniture with hazardous foams could create a lethal atmosphere within about five minutes, if a ground floor living room door was left open. Detailed examination of actual fires revealed that people often had less than two minutes to escape downstairs after the discovery of a fire. If they had not escaped by then, death was very likely[2].

## Human behaviour in fires

Few people have experience of being involved in a fire and are therefore poorly prepared. A study by the Building Research Establishment suggests that although some people do have a clear idea of what action to take in a fire, it cannot be taken for granted that they will act logically and rationally[3]. For instance:

● People may ignore or misunderstand strange noises or smells. These signs often
  indicate the early stages of a fire. Misinterpretation is more of a danger in
  multiply-occupied dwelling fires because occupants may not know each other;
  may not know whether other people are at home or be able to investigate

2. Silcock, A. et al. (1978) *Fires in dwellings – an investigation of actual fires,* Building Research Establishment
3. Canter, D. (1985) *Studies of Human Behaviour in Fire: Empirical Results and their Implications for Education and Design,* Building Research Establishment Report BR61

suspicious signs because they do not have access to other dwellings in the building.

- If the unusual signs continue, people often go to investigate but then return to where they came from, rather than quickly getting out.

- People may attempt to pack, dress or gather belongings.

- People may attempt to contact others or to discuss the situation.

- Once the seriousness of the situation is appreciated, warning others, contacting the fire brigade and escape become high priorities. However, individuals may be unsure as to who knows about the fire and may not phone 999 because they think others have done so.

# Risks of injury or death from fire

In 1997, the Government published information about the fire risks in houses in multiple occupation (HMOs). This confirmed that the risk of being injured or killed in a fire depends on a number of factors relating to the building and the way it is occupied.

### Type of building

The 1997 research showed that rates of fire deaths in some types of HMO are greater than in similar houses in single occupation. It also suggested that fatality rates in flats, whether converted or purpose-built, are higher than in houses.

When comparing the rates of death per person, per year it was found that:

- Adults who live in bedsits are six times more likely to die in a fire than adults living in comparable single-occupancy houses.

- Elderly people living in purpose-built HMOs (e.g. residential care homes) are three times more likely to die in a fire than elderly people living in comparable single-occupancy houses.

- Households living in houses converted into self-contained flats are over two and a half times more likely to die in a fire than households living in comparable single-occupancy houses.

- Households living in hostels are over twice as likely to die in a fire than households living in comparable single-occupancy houses.

- Households living in single-occupancy, purpose-built flats are also twice as likely to die in a fire than households living in comparable single-occupancy houses.

- People living in shared houses and households with lodgers face approximately the same risks as those living in single-occupancy houses.

The way that a building is occupied is only one factor influencing the risk to life from fire; the risk will also vary depending on the number of storeys. The 1997 research showed that the rates of fire deaths in HMOs increased dramatically if the building was over two storeys high. For example, 52% of HMO fire deaths occur in buildings of three or more storeys high, even though only 16.5% of HMO households live in such buildings. One explanation is that, on a higher floor, people are more likely to become trapped because it is more difficult to escape safely through a window or down a stairwell filled with smoke and fumes.

Figure 5 shows that in particular types of higher storey HMO, the risk of being killed in a fire increases even more. For example, the fatality rate in houses of three or more storeys converted into self-contained flats is over five and a half times greater than for the same dwellings in buildings of less than three storeys.

**Figure 5: Percentage risk of death from fire per person per year in HMOs**

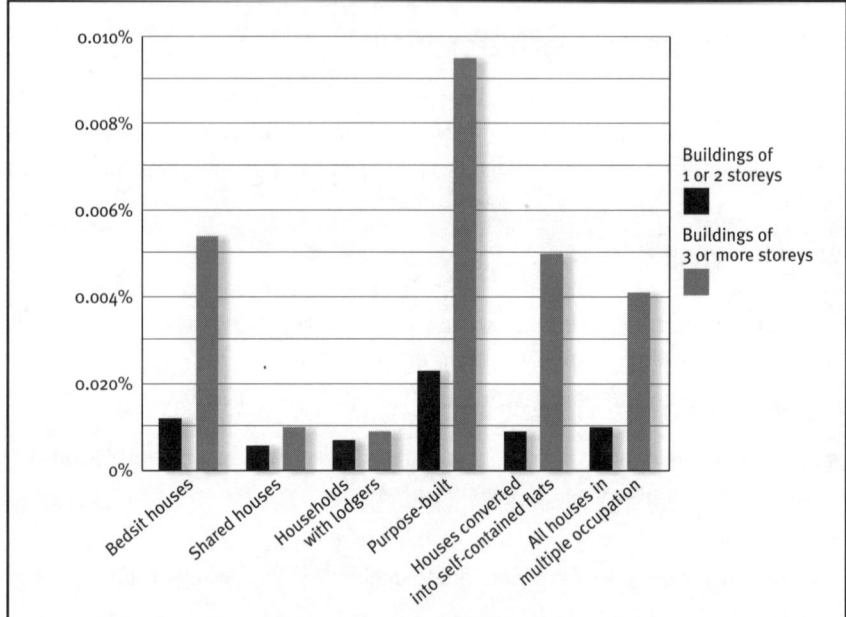

(Source: Department of the Environment, Transport & the Regions (1997) Fire Risk in Houses in Multiple Occupation: Research Report)

When fire death rates in HMOs above three storeys are then compared to the rates in single-occupancy dwellings, the risk to life from fire is greater still. For example, an adult living in a bedsit house of three or more storeys is almost 17 times more likely to be killed in a fire than an adult living in a single-occupancy house.

People living in HMOs clearly face additional dangers as cookers are often old and shared; space heaters may be portable and electrical wiring is often old and in need of replacement, or has been extended in a hazardous way.

## Number & type of occupants

The research on HMO fire risks concluded that the higher fatality rates in such buildings could be linked, in part, to the fact that they often have a higher number of occupants. This means that there may be a greater likelihood of a serious fire occurring, and people being trapped in such a fire, in buildings accommodating larger numbers of people.

The age of occupants may also be a factor contributing to the risk of being killed or injured in a residential fire. Figure 6 illustrates that whilst more elderly people are killed by fire, all age groups are at risk of injury.

**Figure 6: Deaths and injuries from fires in all dwellings by age, UK, 1997**

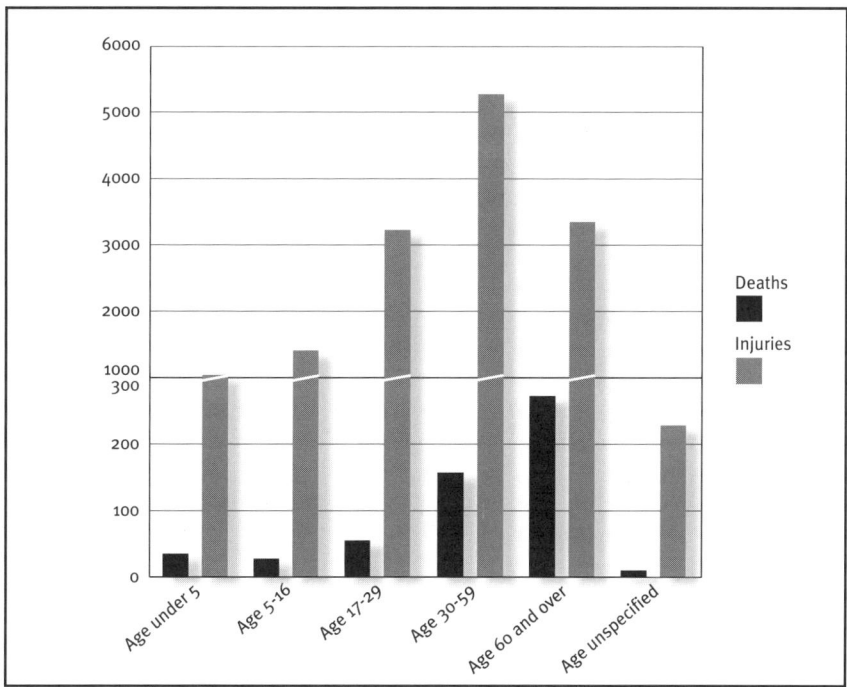

(Source: Government Statistical Service (1998) Fire Statistics, United Kingdom, 1997)

The 1997 research on fire risks in HMOs showed that the vast majority of deaths in purpose-built HMOs and hostels involve elderly people whose clothing, bedding or seat covers were ignited by cigarettes or other smoking materials.

This illustrates that the risk of serious injury or death from a fire may be linked to the nature of the occupants. The research concludes that the ability of persons to react to a fire, or to attempt escape, is influenced by their vulnerability. Occupants who may be at greater risk include:

- children (under 10 years of age)
- elderly (over 60 years of age)
- physically infirm
- mentally ill
- psychologically distressed
- under the influence of alcohol or drugs (including medication)

The type of occupants may also add to the risk of a fire being caused deliberately. The DETR research suggests that the nature of occupancy and whether it is a particular target of arson can influence the likelihood of a serious fire occurring. For instance, the research found that arson attacks account for over 33% of fatal fires in hostels.

# What you can do to prevent a fire starting or spreading

## Cooking with fat or oil (e.g. chip pans)

- Never fill a pan more than a third full of fat or oil.
- Never put food in the pan without drying the food, or if the oil is smoking.
- Never leave the pan unattended.

## Fire and heaters

- Always place a guard around an open fire.
- Never sit closer than three feet (1m) to a heater.
- Never put clothes, furnishings or anything flammable near a fire or heater.
- Always switch off portable heaters before going to bed, unless they are thermostatically controlled.

## Smoking

- Never leave a cigarette or pipe unattended.
- Never smoke in bed, and never smoke in an armchair if you think you might doze off.
- Never leave matches or lighters within the reach of children.
- Never empty an ashtray into the bin unless the contents are cold.

## Electrics

- Always switch off and unplug all electric appliances after use (apart from those that are designed to stay on), especially before you go to bed.
- Do not overload plug sockets with adapters or extension leads.

## Candles

- Never leave a burning candle unattended.
- Never leave a candle burning if you think you might fall asleep.
- Never place a burning candle near anything flammable (curtains, furnishings, books).

- Never leave a burning candle in a draught.

- Always ensure that candles are placed on a stable, non-flammable stand.

## Smoke alarms

- In 1997, 69% of dwelling fires were discovered by a smoke alarm in less than five minutes[4]. As an absolute minimum preventative measure, occupants should ensure that a smoke alarm (with the British Standard kitemark) is fitted correctly in the hallway and on each upstairs landing of their homes. Although the installation of alarms is the landlord's responsibility, providing your own basic alarm whilst waiting for your landlord to fit the correct fire warning system could save your life.

## What to do if there is a fire

- Use your time wisely and try not to panic.

- Try to think clearly about how you might escape. It will help if you are familiar with, and have planned, your possible escape routes.

- Never put yourself in any danger.

- Only attempt to put out a fire in its very early stages.

- Never enter a building to rescue someone trapped by fire.

### If a pan catches fire:

Do not move it.

Turn off the heat, but only if you can do this safely, then cover the pan with a damp cloth or tea towel, or fire blanket, and leave it to cool for at least 30 minutes.

Never throw water on to the fire. If you are unsure how to put out a chip pan fire, do not try. Instead, leave the room, close the door and call the fire service.

 4 Government Statistical Service (1998) Fire Statistics, United Kingdom, 1997

## GET OUT!

Make sure that people are alerted as quickly as possible, preferably by an alarm.

Get everyone out of the building. Do not waste time collecting valuables.

Close all doors behind you, especially the door of the room where the fire is. This will help delay the spread of fire and smoke.

Do not open a closed door if it feels warm. The fire could be behind it. Check the temperature of the door (but not the handle) with the back of your hand.

## CALL THE FIRE BRIGADE OUT!

Phone the fire service by dialling 999 and clearly state the location of the fire.

Wait outside in a safe place until the fire service arrives. It is important that people know where you are so that lives are not put at risk trying to find you, and so that the fire service can ask you about other occupants or the layout of the building.

## STAY OUT!

Do not go back into the building for any reason.

**If you are trapped by the fire:** Remember that smoke is as deadly as flames. If possible, go to a room facing the road, close the door and use bedding or other material to block any gaps which might let in smoke or fumes.

Open the window. If it is jammed, break it with a piece of furniture. Carefully remove jagged glass from the lower sill and cover it with a blanket.

Attract someone's attention from the window. Make sure that the fire service has been called. They should arrive very quickly. In the meantime, wait by the window.

If the room becomes smoky, stay low as it will be easier to breath.

If you are certain that you are in immediate danger, and the room is not too far from the ground, drop cushions or bedding to break your fall. If you can, get out feet first and lower yourself to the full length of your arms before dropping. You should never attempt to drop more than two storeys.

If it is too dangerous to escape from a window, wait for the fire service to rescue you.

**If someone's clothes are on fire:**

Get them to lie on the floor and roll them in blankets, rugs or a thick coat.

If your clothes catch fire, roll on the floor to extinguish the flames and quickly remove any bits of burned material that are not touching your skin.

# 2 Identifying fire safety standards

Having read Chapter 1, you should be aware of how most fires start and spread. You should also be aware that the risk of a fire causing death, injury or serious damage can depend on the type of building and the way it is occupied. The law reflects this by requiring specific fire safety standards in those dwellings considered most at risk: houses in multiple occupation (HMOs). However, there are a number of different categories of HMO to which different levels of fire safety apply.

Therefore, if you are worried about fire safety in your dwelling and want to check whether the current fire safety standards meet the legal requirements, you must:

- establish whether the dwelling is an HMO and, if it is

- establish what category of HMO the dwelling falls into for fire safety purposes.

> The definition of an HMO and the categories for fire safety standards are a very complicated area of the law. The aim of this chapter is to help most people decide which fire safety standards are required in their dwellings. If you are still confused about whether the dwelling is an HMO, or which category it falls into, do not be put off − lives could be at risk. Contact your local council's Environmental Health Department or seek housing advice[5].

## Definition of an HMO

Deciding whether a particular dwelling is an HMO is easy in some cases, but very difficult in others. It relies on legal definitions and past court cases. In general, a dwelling in which facilities (e.g. kitchen, bathroom) are shared by more than one 'household' is usually classified as an HMO. In addition, some dwellings with no shared facilities (e.g. houses converted into self-contained flats) are also classified as HMOs. To make matters more confusing, there has recently been much legal debate over the definition of a 'household'. For more information on the definition of an HMO, see Appendix A.

## Fire safety standards in non-HMOs

In singly-occupied dwellings (e.g. houses occupied by only one household), there are no specific fire safety standards required by the law other than the Building Regulations, which set standards depending on the type of dwelling. However, these cannot be applied to all buildings (see page 69). In addition, any dwelling which is in

5 See Appendix B

such a poor state that it is considered unfit for human habitation[6] may attract local authority attention, and works may be required to make it fit. Government guidance[7] states that when deciding whether a dwelling is fit for human habitation, 'the primary concern should lie in safeguarding the health and safety of any occupants'. Although there is no criterion specified for fire safety, premises without adequate provision may fail the fitness standard under other criteria. For instance, items of serious disrepair which might cause a fire (e.g. faulty electrical wiring) or might prevent occupants from escaping from the fire (e.g. windows or doors which are jammed shut) would not usually be considered acceptable standards of fitness.

Therefore, if you are sure that your dwelling cannot be classified as an HMO, it should still be fit enough to safeguard against serious risks to fire safety. However, it is necessary to emphasise that interpretation of the standards of fitness can vary widely, depending on the severity of the defects and the likely harm they may cause.

## Sources of fire safety standards in HMOs

The standards set out in this chapter and chapter 3 are based on a number of different pieces of guidance to local authorities, which are responsible for setting and enforcing standards in private rented accommodation. All of the guidance is advisory and so local authorities may choose to enforce higher or lower standards. This is why the required standards sometimes differ locally. However, if a landlord provides lower standards than those contained in the guidance, and the local authority accepts them, both may have to give a detailed justification for this in the face of a legal challenge.

### Government HMO guidance

In 1992, the Government issued detailed guidance to local authorities on the standards they might consider adopting when exercising their enforcement powers under certain sections of the Housing Act 1985[8]. This includes guidance on standards for means of escape from fire and other fire precautions. In April 1999, the Government acknowledged that the 1992 guidance may no longer be appropriate in all cases, in the light of the findings of the DETR research, *Fire Risk in HMOs,* quoted in Chapter 1. However, for a variety of reasons, the Government envisaged that it may be some time before new standards could be issued. Consequently, revised guidance was issued to local authorities as an interim measure[9]. This guidance stated that: 'It is now a generally accepted principle within Government that health and safety standards should be goal based and related to risk'. It is clear that future guidance from the Government will be based on analysing the fire risk in each HMO. Meanwhile, local authorities are already being encouraged to use this approach.

6. Housing Act 1985, Section 604. 7. Department of the Environment Circular No.17/96 *Private Sector Renewal: a Strategic Approach.* 8. Department of the Environment Circular 12/92, *Houses in Multiple Occupation: Guidance to local housing authorities on standards of fitness under section 352 of the Housing Act 1985.* 9. Department of the Environment, Transport and the Regions: Letter to local authorities, dated 28 April 1999, *Houses in Multiple Occupation: Guidance on Standards.*

## Government hotel guidance

The Government also provides guidance on acceptable standards for obtaining a fire certificate for hotels and boarding houses[10]. A separate, non-technical guide for hotel owners and managers, based on the Government hotel guidance, is available[11].

## British Standards

The law does not specifically require that British Standards are applied when building work is carried out or fire precautions are installed. However, in legal proceedings they will be relied on to provide an independent standard for the quality of work or fire safety precautions. They also represent good standards to aim for and provide professional guidance on technical topics. When an environmental health professional (or other person) specifies that some work should be carried out, or a fire warning system is installed, they may often require it to meet a particular British Standard. This helps to achieve a clear, unambiguous standard for that work.

There are many British Standards relating to fire safety. The most recent British Standard on fire safety in homes is BS5839: Part 6: 1995[12]. It covers HMOs that are described as 'dwellings' (this excludes hostels, boarding houses and hotels). It advises that any HMO should be assessed for its fire risk and then all work should be based on the level of risk that is found. The four main factors that must be considered are:

1. the probability of a fire occurring

2. the probability of injury or death of occupants if a fire occurs

3. the probability of the fire alarm system operating correctly at the time of a fire

4. the probability of early detection and warning of occupants in the event of fire.

## Chartered Institute of Environmental Health (CIEH) Guides

Two guides have been published by the Chartered Institute of Environmental Health.

The first is what we call the *CIEH (London) Guide*[13]. This has been issued to every London borough and is in use by over 100 local authorities in the UK as well as the London Fire Brigade. It provides a wealth of technical details on all aspects of fire safety in HMOs, especially recommending in great detail different fire warning systems for different types of HMOs.

The second guide, referred to in this book as the *CIEH (Greater Manchester) Guide*[14], was published by a working group of Greater Manchester local authorities with advice from many fire experts. It provides fewer technical details but gives considerable assistance in interpreting the legal requirements and the Government advice.

Both guides are recommended to anyone wishing to investigate fuller technical details or explanations of particular points. Neither guide has any legal force but in a legal case, or any other dispute, they can be used as evidence of adequate and acceptable standards.

10. Home Office/Scottish Office (1991) *Guide to fire precautions in premises used as hotels and boarding houses which require a fire certificate.* 11. (1991) *Fire Safety Management in Hotels and Boarding Houses.* 12. British Standard 5839: Part 6: 1995, *Fire detection and alarm systems for buildings (Part 6: Code of practice for the design and installation of fire detection and alarm systems) in dwellings.* 13 Chartered Institute of Environmental Health (1997) *Fire precautions for houses in multiple occupation: a practical and technical guide.* 14. Chartered Institute of Environmental Health (1995) *Fire safety for houses in multiple occupation: an illustrated guide.*

## Common fire safety standards for all HMOs

There are certain fire safety features that should be common to all HMOs. These include:

○ No unsafe electrical wiring

○ A basic fire warning system

○ An escape route, free from obstructions or materials that burn easily

○ No portable ladders or similar devices used as a means of escape

○ Good maintenance and repair of all means of escape and fire precautions

○ Locks on exit doors which can be opened easily without a key

○ Fire extinguishers and fire blanket(s) in shared kitchens

○ Fire resistant furniture and furnishings (see Chapter 4, pages 70-71).

If the HMOs are three storeys high or more, or are larger and have a more complex layout, then additional fire safety measures will be required:

○ More complex requirements for escape routes and fire warning systems

○ No long travel distances within rooms to a means of escape

○ Escape lighting depending on the exact layout and complexity of the building

○ Fire notices, where the escape route is not the normal route of travel, or where there might be any doubt about the location of the exit(s)

○ Safe surface finishes to walls and ceilings

○ A fire resistant floor between any basement and ground floor

○ Any external fire escape must be protected from potential fire and smoke.

## Categories of HMO for fire safety purposes

If you have established that your dwelling is likely to be classified as an HMO, then you need to work out what category it falls into for fire safety purposes. There are six main categories:

● Houses converted into self-contained flats, each occupied by a single household

● Shared houses and Bedsit type houses

● Shared flats (Flats in Multiple Occupation)

● Houses containing a mixture of flats in single occupation and bedsits

● Hostels

● Hotels and Boarding houses

Within these categories, there are different fire safety standards depending mainly on the number of storeys in the building. The two features that change the most, according to the height and type of HMO, are the requirements for fire warning systems and fire escape. These changing requirements are set out below together with the other main safety features you would expect to have in these different HMOs.

For a more detailed explanation of these standards, see Chapter 3.

# Houses converted into self contained flats, each occupied by a single household[15]

## Up to 2 storeys

### Fire warning systems
Government HMO guidance recommends mains powered smoke alarms as a minimum. The British Standard[16] states these should be linked so that they all sound when any one alarm is triggered.

The *CIEH (London) Guide* recommends that smoke alarms should be installed within the staircase, landings, halls and any lobby or hallway areas, including those inside each flat. If there is not an internal lobby or hallway area within the flat then a smoke alarm should be installed in the room next to the staircase. A Grade E system is recommended. The *CIEH (Greater Manchester) Guide* adds that smoke alarms should be fitted in all bedrooms, cellars and storage areas and the common areas.

### Fire escape
The original Government HMO guidance in 1992 recommended that the stairway and any associated exit route must be a protected escape route and that the floor between the ground and first floor must also be fire resistant. However, current guidance states that, due to the lower risk of death or injury, this is not necessary in one or two storey HMOs, providing the following conditions are met:

- there are less than six occupants
- all habitable rooms have an openable window or door for escape purposes
- there are no bedsits
- no habitable room can only be accessed through another room
- all rooms have close fitting internal doors
- there are no other adverse risk factors.

## 3 - 6 storeys

### Fire warning systems
The original Government HMO guidance recommended an Automatic Fire Detection L2 fire warning system which met BS 5839:Part 1:1988. The more recent British Standard (BS 5839:Part 6:1995) recommends that the risks are analysed before deciding exactly what is needed.

The *CIEH (London) Guide* recommends that, in 'standard risk' premises, there should be a Grade A system with smoke detectors throughout the staircase, hallways, landings and any lobbies. If lobbies are present, then no smoke detectors are required in rooms leading off the staircase. However, where no lobby is present,

---

smoke detectors (or heat detectors if the room is used for cooking) should be installed in rooms next to the staircase unless they are bathrooms or WC compartments. There should be a control panel and manual call points on each storey. Alarm sounders will be needed to provide a minimum 75 decibels at each bedhead (i.e. usually in each bedroom).

The *CIEH (Greater Manchester) Guide* recommends a similar system to the above in the communal areas. In the self-contained accommodation it recommends Grade D interlinked smoke and heat alarms.

## Fire escape

The stairway and any associated exit route must be a protected escape route and all floors must also be fire resistant. Travel distances from the accommodation exit to the nearest stairways must not exceed the maximum standards.

If there are five or six storeys, the Government HMO guidance states that a single, internal staircase is only acceptable if three conditions are met:

- the stairway is a protected escape route, and

- all the accommodation is separated from the stairway by means of protected lobbies, and

- in houses with no more than six storeys, a suitable upward escape route, which terminates at a safe final exit, is available within the existing stairway.

# Shared houses[17] and Bedsit type houses

## Up to 2 storeys

### Fire warning systems

Government HMO guidance recommends mains powered smoke alarms as a minimum. The British Standard[18] states that these should be linked so that they all sound when any one alarm is triggered. There need be no stand-by power supply.

Both CIEH Guides recommend that smoke alarms which are interlinked should cover the staircase, landings, halls, lobby area, living rooms, bedrooms and bedsit areas. Heat detectors will be needed in rooms where cooking takes place.

The *CIEH (London) Guide* recommends that in any bedsits containing cooking facilities, there should be heat detectors. There should also be a smoke alarm with a battery back-up (wired to the lighting circuit but not linked to other alarms) set to only sound in that bedsit area. The idea is to make sure any false alarms set off by cooking in that bedsit only results in a noisy alarm affecting that area.

### Fire escape

The same standards are recommended as for houses converted into self-contained flats, up to two storeys high (see page 21). The escape route from the first floor must be a protected route built of fire resisting materials and with fire doors.

## 3 - 6 storeys

### Fire warning systems

The original Government HMO guidance recommends an Automatic Fire Detection L2 system which meets BS 5839:Part 1: 1988.

The more recent British Standard (BS 5839:Part 6: 1995) recommends that the risks are analysed before deciding exactly what is needed.

The *CIEH (London) Guide* recommends that, in 'standard risk' premises, there should be a Grade A system with LD2 coverage. Consequently, there should be smoke detectors covering the staircase, landings, hallways and lobbies as well as the living rooms, bedrooms and bedsit areas. There should be a control panel in the ground floor hallway and manual call points on all floors. Heat detectors will be needed in rooms where cooking takes place.

The *CIEH (London) Guide* also recommends a heat detector in any bedsits containing cooking facilities. There should be a smoke alarm with a battery back-up (wired to the lighting circuit but not linked to other alarms) set to only sound in that bedsit area. The idea is to make sure any false alarms set off by cooking in that bedsit only results in a noisy alarm affecting that bedsit area.

### Fire escape

The same standards are recommended as for houses converted into self-contained flats, which are three to six storeys high (see page 22).

17. It is important to read Appendix A in relation to the definition of shared houses as HMOs. 18. British Standard 5839:Part 6:1995.

# Shared flats (Flats in Multiple Occupation)

The *CIEH (London) Guide* is the only guide to set out which standards apply to flats in multiple occupation (FMOs). It recommends the following:

## FMOs located within purpose-built blocks (i.e. mansion blocks)

Mains wired smoke alarms should be provided. These should be linked so that they all sound when any one alarm is triggered. No stand-by power is necessary. There should be interlinked smoke alarms in the internal hallway or lobby of the flat, as well as interlinked smoke alarms in the bedrooms and living rooms. There should also be an interlinked heat alarm in the kitchen.

## FMOs located within a converted house which also contains bedsits

The standards relating to bedsit houses should apply.

## FMOs located within a house converted only into self-contained flats

The standards relating to self-contained flats should apply. In addition, for the FMO flat, the following additional work should be carried out to the automatic fire detection system:

### Up to 2 storeys

Mains wired smoke alarms which are linked so that they all sound when any one alarm is triggered. No stand-by power is necessary. There should be interlinked smoke alarms to the staircase, landings, hallways and lobbies as well as interlinked smoke alarms to bedrooms and living rooms. There should be heat alarms in kitchens.

### 3-6 storeys

An LD2 (Grade A) Automatic Fire Detection system should be extended into the FMO communal kitchen, living room and bedrooms. There should be smoke detectors in the hallway, living room and bedrooms. There should be a heat detector in the kitchen.

# Houses containing a mixture of flats in single occupation and bedsit accommodation

## Up to 2 storeys

### Fire warning systems

The *CIEH (Greater Manchester) Guide* recommends interlinked smoke alarms on the escape routes and, according to risk, in bedrooms, living rooms and storage areas.

The *CIEH (London) Guide* recommends that, in these situations, its guidance for flats in single occupation and bedsit type HMOs should be followed. Generally, this would result in a Grade E system of smoke and heat alarms, covering:

- stairway enclosure
- lobbies and internal hallways of flats
- bedsits.

## 3 - 6 storeys

### Fire warning systems

The *CIEH (Greater Manchester) Guide* recommends the following. If the units of accommodation do not have entrance lobbies then these units and the common areas should be fitted with an Automatic Fire Detection LD2 Grade A system.

If there are units of bedsit accommodation with cooking facilities leading off the common hallway, they should have a heat detector linked to an LD2 Grade A system. They should also have an individual smoke alarm unconnected to the main alarm system, which will alarm the bedsit area only.

If the units of accommodation have an entrance lobby then there should be a smoke detector in this lobby area and an alarm sounder in the bedroom linked to the LD2 system. At the same time there should be individual smoke detectors (or heat detectors where cooking takes place) wired into the mains and all interlinked, namely a Grade D system. The idea here is that there are two basic fire alarm systems. One that covers the whole building and links with the entrance lobby and provides a sounder in the bedroom. The other that just covers that unit of accommodation and gives the occupants warning of a fire in their own accommodation.

The *CIEH (London) Guide* recommends a grade A system, covering:

- stairway enclosure
- lobbies and internal hallways of flats
- bedsits.

# Hostels

## 2-6 storeys

### Fire warning systems

The Government HMO guidance and the *CIEH (London) Guide* recommend an Automatic Fire Detection L2 system which meets BS 5839:Part 1:1988 in all hostels. Consequently, there should be smoke detectors covering the staircase, landings, hallways and lobbies. Each room (except bathrooms or WCs) leading off a staircase should also have a smoke detector, as should any other risk rooms (e.g. bedrooms or living rooms). Heat detectors will be needed in rooms where cooking takes place. Alarm sounders will be needed to provide a minimum 75 decibels at each bedhead (i.e. usually in each bedroom).

### Fire escape

The escape route from the first floor must be a protected route built of fire resisting materials and with fire doors or a very similar arrangement. There should also be protected lobbies.

#### Stairways

Like protected escape routes, all hostel stairway enclosures must be separated from the rest of the building by fire resisting materials and fire doors. Ideally stairway enclosures should lead directly to a final exit but sometimes this is not possible. If there is only one stairway then two alternative solutions exist.

- Two exits can be provided from this stairway which give access to routes (possibly corridors) leading to two final exits. These routes must be separated from each other by fire resisting construction.

- A protected route can be made to link the stairway with a final exit. For instance, a stairway may end in a large entrance lobby. If the whole of this lobby becomes a protected route, then people can cross it to reach the main exit door.

The Government HMO guidance states that, for fire escape purposes in hostels, 'ideally more than one stairway should be provided'. If this is not possible for structural or layout reasons, a single stairway is satisfactory, provided:

- the floor area of any upper storeys does not exceed 200 square metres and maximum distances of travel are not exceeded (see pages 50-51).

- the house has no more than four floors or, if it does have more, no upper floor is at a height of more than 11 metres above ground level.

- the stairway system is designed to the stairway enclosure guidelines (described above).

- if the hostel is more than two storeys high, then access to the stairway from any room should be through two sets of fire doors (unless it is a toilet without fire risk). Or, if this is not practical, an alternative method can be used in a building which does not exceed three storeys. Fire doors can be fitted to all rooms opening on to the stairway and an automatic fire warning system must be installed.

- there should also be 'adequate fire risk management' (i.e. the fact that there are only single fire doors and a single escape route should be taken in to account and additional precautions considered, such as a more extensive alarm system).

- the house has five or six storeys and there are suitable upward escape routes.

## Corridors

In hostels, all corridors connected to sleeping accommodation and all corridors which form dead ends, must be of fire resisting construction and all doors to the corridors should be fire doors. If a single corridor branches out into two alternative escape routes, self-closing fire doors should separate off the two alternative routes.

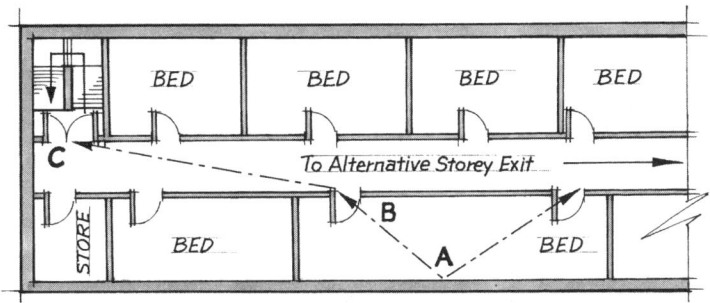

*Distance of Travel A·B·C not Exceeding 35m    Distance of Travel A·B not Exceeding 18m*

If corridors are longer than 30 metres, they should be divided up to restrict smoke travelling the length of the corridor. Self-closing doors, which do not need to be fire doors, can be provided for this purpose. They must be of substantial construction and fitted with smoke seals.

## Other

- Travel distances from rooms to a stairway or a final exit and within stairways must not exceed the maximum.

- Escape lighting is required.

## Fire instruction and fire drills

The Government HMO guidance requires hostel staff to be instructed at least twice a year in fire safety, including what to do if they discover a fire, or hear a fire alarm. As a result of this training, staff should know:

- all the escape routes

- the location of, and how to use, all fire fighting equipment, alarm points and alarm indicator panels

- how to call the fire brigade.

Except in 'small' hostels there should be fire drills twice a year. A written record should be kept of all drills and training. Residents should be made aware of evacuation procedures and encouraged to take part in drills. Every bedroom and other parts of a hostel should have clear printed notices, stating the correct procedure if an alarm goes off, or a fire is discovered. They should show where to assemble. Instructions should be provided in the languages most commonly used by residents.

# Hotels and Boarding houses

Any hotel and boarding house where board and lodging is provided for more than six people should be covered by a fire certificate. The standards set out below are based on the Government hotel guidance, unless otherwise stated.

## Fire warning systems

For all new fire certificates, or where the premises are 'materially altered', or where there is a change of use and the fire certificate needs amendments, there should be an Automatic Fire Detection L2 system.

Where it is not possible to meet other standards of fire safety, an L1 system covering the whole building is recommended.

> However, the Government hotel guidance effectively supports lower standards than local authorities can demand, since it argues that where the premises already have a fire certificate there is no basis in law for demanding such an L2 system. This is because standards cannot be backdated prior to the guidance. It does say, however, that fire authorities can point out that previous systems do not meet current standards, but cannot legally require a change. This position can be overcome in practice in HMOs. If the fire authority cannot demand higher standards, the local council can step in and use their powers under Section 352 of the Housing Act 1985 to demand a full L2 system. Local authorities have a legal right to require improvements to systems which may have been considered satisfactory a few years ago.

The Government hotel guidance acknowledges that detectors sited solely in corridors could be inadequate, under certain circumstances, for the protection of escape routes. Smoke detectors should be placed in sleeping accommodation. They should also be placed in dormitory type accommodation even where it is divided into cubicles. Domestic smoke detectors are not acceptable.

Intercoms or public address systems should be used in the event of fire and 'consideration should be given' to pre-prepared messages in different languages.

## Fire escape

### Exits

At least two exits must be provided to large rooms, occupied by more than 60 people, where the distances of travel are exceeded. The width, siting and number of exits must be carefully calculated. If one of the largest exits is put out of action by a fire, there must be sufficient other exits for people to escape safely. So any exits should be as widely spaced as possible and lead to distinct and separate exit routes.

### Corridors

All corridors serving sleeping accommodation, and all corridors where there is escape in one direction only, should be protected escape routes. Corridors should normally be at least 1.05m wide and, if they exceed 30m in length, be sub-divided by smoke control doors.

### Stairways

There should normally be two stairways but a single stairway may be considered satisfactory where:

1. The floor area of any upper floors does not exceed 200 square metres

2. The travel distances (see chapter 3) are not exceeded

3. The building has no more than four floors or no upper floor is at a height of more than 11 metres

4. In buildings of three or more storeys, the stairway must be reached from any room (excluding a toilet with no fire risk) through two sets of fire doors

5. The stairway leads directly to the final exit or, if this is not possible:

a) either there should be two exits from the stairway, each giving access to final exits, and the two routes must be separated from each other by fire resisting construction, or

b) there must be a protected route leading from the foot of the stairs to a final exit.

Where an external stairway is provided it must be a protected route. This means it cannot be affected by smoke or flames from doors or windows in the external wall next to this external stairway. The stairway should have lighting and be protected from the weather.

### Upward escape routes

Escape in an upwards direction to a roof is not generally considered satisfactory. Conditions are placed on the use of such escape routes. Escape using intercommunication doors is only considered satisfactory where a binding agreement is in force between all interested parties so that the route is always available. Portable and throw-out ladders, lowering lines and rope ladders are not considered suitable. Fixed vertical and sloping ladders are only suitable for active, able-bodied staff. They must provide an escape to a final exit (i.e. to the street).

### Other

- All escape routes, both internal and external, including stairways, should be provided with both normal and emergency electrical systems.

- Maximum travel distance times must not be exceeded.

- Surface finishes in circulation areas and escape routes must be of the highest level of fire resistance (i.e. comprise of special fire-resisting boards).

## Fire Instruction and Drills

The Government hotel guidance extends the advice given on hostels by emphasising a duty to train staff, which can be required as part of a fire certificate.

Night staff should be trained at three-monthly intervals, day-time staff at six monthly intervals. Instruction and training should be based on written procedures.

New staff, cleaners and casual workers should be shown means of escape and told the fire routine as soon as possible. Training must be designed to take account of any limited knowledge of English in members of staff.

In larger hotels, managers should have a written action plan. A detailed building plan, showing key features relevant for the fire brigade, should be kept in all but the smallest premises.

## Fire fighting

The type, location and number of fire extinguishers, fire blankets or hose reels will be recorded on the fire certificate.

Printed notices, including floor plans, should be displayed at conspicuous positions throughout the building (e.g. hotel bedrooms, public rooms). All notices should be fixed permanently and laminated or framed to protect them. The details of fire notices should be recorded on the fire certificate.

## Floor coverings, furniture and furnishings, beds and bedding

Furniture, furnishings, beds, bedding and synthetic materials should comply with the Furniture and Furnishings Regulations[19].

Floor coverings should conform to the relevant British Standard[20] since some floor coverings can release large volumes of smoke and heat.

Curtains should also meet the relevant British Standard and not conceal notices or be hung in front of fire exit doors[21]

## Maintenance

A fire certificate places a duty on hotel or boarding house management to maintain:

- the means of escape

- a system for alerting staff and guests to any fire

- the fire fighting equipment.

A fire certificate will normally require a fire logbook to be kept, which would include fire drill details, training and maintenance of equipment.

## Special measures for people with disabilities

Special steps need to be taken for people with disabilities. The Government hotel guidance provides further details and references for further advice.

19. Furniture and Furnishings (Fire) (Safety) Regulations 1988 and Furniture and Furnishings (Fire) (Safety) Amendment Regulations 1989. 20. BS 5287:1988 *Specification for assessment and labeling of textile floor coverings tested to BS 4790.* 21. Curtains should conform with BS 5867: Part 2 fabric type B when tested in accordance with British Standard 5438.

# 3 Fundamentals of fire safety

Having read Chapter 2, you should be aware of what fire safety standards are required in your dwelling. This chapter explains the key components in detail. The aim is to explain the purpose of each element of fire safety, including what should happen in practice.

## This chapter is divided into three sections:

### 1. Fire warning
This includes fire detection and alarm systems.

### 2. Fire escape
This includes protected escape routes and lobbies; fire resistance; surface finishes; distance of travel; internal layout; fire doors; escape lighting and escape notices.

### 3. Fire fighting
This includes fire extinguishers and fire blankets.

## Section 1: FIRE WARNING

In the past decade, awareness of the value of smoke alarms has rapidly increased. We have moved from just a few alarms in homes to hundreds of thousands being voluntarily installed. However, there is now a growing awareness of the quality of the alarms being fitted, and how alarm systems (particularly cheap battery-powered alarms) can fail when they are needed.

## What is a fire warning system?

The purpose of a fire warning system is to make occupants aware there is a fire, leaving enough time for them to escape before the protected escape routes are blocked by fire and smoke. There are two main functions involved in warning occupants of a fire:

- detection of the fire, smoke or fumes

- raising the alarm.

### Automatic fire detection and alarm
These systems detect a fire and raise the alarm automatically, without any human assistance. A detector, containing a sensor (or, in some circumstances, two sensors) is a crucial part of an automatic system. The sensor monitors constantly for any

physical or chemical signs indicating a fire. When a fire is detected, the alarm is raised by means of a sounder. Cheap, individual smoke alarms contain both a detector and a sounder and are available at all DIY stores. However, HMOs almost always need more sophisticated automatic fire detection and alarm systems (AFDs), where the detectors are usually separate from the sounders.

## Manual fire alarm systems

These contain no automatic detectors. Instead, they rely on people to detect the fire and raise the alarm at a manual call point (e.g. a little red box where you break the glass), which activates the sounder. Consequently, manual systems are only effective if occupants are present and awake, and have been trained on using the equipment. As these factors cannot be guaranteed, manual fire alarm systems should never be used as the only means of warning occupants of a fire. However, manual call points can form part of an automatic system, allowing people to raise the alarm before a detector is triggered.

In most HMOs where there is a higher risk of fire, fire warning systems should include a combination of both automatic fire detectors and manual call points, therefore ensuring the best chance of the alarm being raised as soon as possible after a fire starts. For example, the Government HMO guidance recommends that both systems are required in all houses of more than two storeys containing self-contained accommodation (with or without shared facilities). Both systems are also required in any hostel-type accommodation with more than one floor (and sometimes in single-storey hostels). In some hotels and boarding houses it is possible to switch the systems to different states of readiness (i.e. a manual system during the day, smoke detectors at night). In larger buildings it may be necessary to group areas into zones, each with its own fire warning system (e.g. each floor may consist of one zone).

# Power supply to fire warning systems

Government HMO guidance states that all fire warning systems should now be powered by mains electricity (previously, the guidance considered that self-contained, battery-operated fire alarms, unconnected to a general alarm system, could be used in some HMOs of one or two storeys).

The guidance does not specifically recommend that alarms should be linked (in other words wired together so that if one alarm goes off then all the alarms in the HMO go off). However, both the CIEH Guides (London and Greater Manchester), and the relevant British Standard, expect smoke and heat detector alarms to be linked, with very few exceptions.

In all but very simple manual alarm systems, it is also necessary to have an alternative source of power in case the mains supply fails. Detectors that are connected to the mains and have a back-up battery which is continually trickle-charged are often used. These are relatively inexpensive, easy to install and have two sources of power.

## Control boxes

Some AFD systems have control boxes. These indicate whether and where an alarm or detector has been triggered. Most importantly, control boxes indicate whether the system is in operation, and should give an audible and visible indication of the presence of any faults on the system. The indicator colours are:

- Red: alarm signal

- Yellow: fault signal

- Green: normal power and working

A control box should be situated in a place near the main entrance, accessible to all the occupants and the fire brigade (e.g. an entrance hall).

## Fire detectors

The actual detector used should conform to the relevant British Standard[22]. There are two main types of detector, heat detectors and smoke detectors, which respond differently to different types of fire.

### Smoke detectors

In general, smoke detectors give a faster response, but they may be subject to more false alarms. A slowly smouldering fire, such as a burning cigarette down the back of an armchair, would probably trigger a smoke detector first. There are two main types of smoke detector:

**Ionisation detectors.** These work by measuring any reduction in an electrical current when smoke particles enter a chamber. They are often a bit quicker to react to hot, blazing fires.

**Optical detectors.** These are better at detecting smoke produced by smouldering fires, but this can lead to false alarms caused by dense tobacco smoke, for instance. However, optical alarms are less likely than ionisation types to be triggered by fumes from cooking and are therefore the most suitable type to use near kitchens. The Government HMO guidance recommends this type where there is no staff supervision.

Both types of smoke detector have a wide range of response and are suitable for general use. Also, there are now products which include both devices in a single unit.

Generally, smoke detectors should be used in the following areas:

- stairways

- corridors

- living rooms

- bedrooms

- stores.

22. British Standard 5445:Part 5:1977; British Standard 5455:Part 7:1984 and/or British Standard 5455:Part 8:1984

## Heat detectors

A fire which rapidly gives off heat but with little smoke, such as some chip pan fires, would trigger a heat detector first. For this reason, heat detectors are unsuitable for escape routes or bedrooms. However, they should be used in areas where steam, condensation or fumes may unnecessarily trigger a smoke alarm, and where there is a higher risk of fire:

- kitchens

- kitchen area in bedsits (backed up with a mains-wired, self-contained smoke alarm in the sleeping area)

- boiler rooms

## Siting of detectors

Detectors should be sited throughout protected escape routes and in any circulation areas. There should be a detector on every landing and they should always be sited at the top of any stairway. In rooms next to the protected escape route, detectors should be sited near the doorway, on the ceiling and 500mm away from the wall. Heat detectors should be between 25mm-150mm of the ceiling surface and smoke detectors should be within 23mm-600mm of the ceiling surface.

# Fire alarms and call points

Manual call points should be clearly identifiable, accessible and simple to use. They should be sited on exit routes and on landings of stairways. No one should have to travel more than 30 metres to reach one.

Alarm sounders (e.g. bells, buzzers) must be capable of waking sleeping people, and so there must be sufficient sounders to make sure they are heard. If sleeping people are to be woken, the minimum level is 75 decibels next to the bed when all the doors are shut (75 decibels is slightly louder than a thunderstorm one or two miles away). The warning signal given by the alarm must be very distinctive – people should not be able to confuse it with any other nearby or familiar sounds.

British Standard 5839[23] states: *'For a fire detection system to give maximum benefit, its alarm should be passed on to the fire brigade with the smallest possible time delay. It may be permissible for the alarm to be passed on by telephone, if there is an adequately trained person on the premises, but frequently the only reliable method will be over an automatic link'*. If there is no such system in an HMO 'the responsibility for calling the fire brigade should both be clearly specified and clearly understood'.

Most HMOs will not have fire alarm systems which automatically alert the fire brigade. Many HMOs are without a communal phone or even a nearby telephone box. Confusion often occurs in a fire with everybody thinking someone else has called the fire brigade. Yet neither the British Standard or the Government HMO guidance requires any access to a telephone. Shelter's Campaign for Bedsit Rights believes that access to a communal phone in all HMOs is an essential fire safety precaution.

## Types of fire warning system

Fire warning systems must follow the recommendations of the current British Standards. These contain detailed standards covering the spacing, siting and areas to be covered by any fire warning system.

- BS 5839: Part 1: 1988 covers fire warning systems in hostels, boarding houses and hotels

- BS 5839: Part 6: 1995[24] covers fire warning systems in most other HMOs

The 1995 British Standard requires that the type of fire warning system used must be based on a detailed risk assessment. It divides systems into two main categories: PD systems aim to protect property, whilst LD systems aim to protect life. LD systems are

23. British Standard 5839:Part1:1988. 24. British Standard 5839: Part 6: 1995, Fire detection and alarm systems for buildings (Part 6: Code of practice for the design and installation of fire detection and alarm systems) in dwellings.

further sub-divided into three different categories:

### LD3 systems

These offer the lowest level of protection. They consist of smoke detectors placed on the escape routes. In HMOs there should be manual call points on exit routes on each storey.

### LD2 systems

These are the same as LD3 systems, but require additional detectors in the 'risk rooms' (e.g. kitchens and living rooms). If the risk assessment justifies it, further detectors should be fixed in other rooms (e.g. bedrooms). In HMOs there should be manual call points on exit routes on each storey.

### LD1 systems

These give the highest coverage of all areas. Heat detectors should be installed in all areas in which smoke detectors might give false alarms and further detectors may be installed (e.g. in some roof voids). In HMOs there should be manual call points on exit routes on each storey.

The most common systems required in HMOs are LD2 and LD3. The types of areas where coverage should be considered are:

- bedrooms
- living rooms
- kitchens
- stairways
- cupboards, storage areas, attics or cellars (where furniture or flammable materials may be stored)
- any other area of high risk.

---

**The difference between LD systems and L systems**

It is important to point out that the British Standard for hostels, boarding houses and hotels uses the descriptions L1, L2 and L3 instead. This is simply because the 1995 British Standard focuses on dwellings (hence LD2), whilst the previous British Standard covered all buildings. There is little substantial difference between the LD and L type systems, except that the LD type is based more on risk analysis. Therefore, although LD and L systems are referred to separately in this guide, they can be considered as broadly similar systems.

---

## Grading of fire warning systems

Fire detection and alarm systems are further sub-divided into grades, which set additional standards (e.g. the quality of the wiring, control panels or control devices, self-monitoring devices and power supplies). There are six grades, ranging from

Grade A (best) to Grade F (most basic).

There is a significant difference in quality between the different Grades. Only three Grades are recommended in the CIEH Guides: Grade A, Grade D and Grade E. The basic differences are:

### Grade A

○ Smoke or heat detectors

○ Sounders

○ Stand-by power for 72 hours in case of power failure

○ Control panel

○ Electrical wiring system protected and automatically monitored for faults

○ Building divided into zones

○ Servicing and testing to meet BS 5839: Part 1: 1988.

### Grade D

○ Mains powered smoke or heat alarms with battery back-up

○ No control panel

○ Unprotected and unmonitored wiring system

○ No zone division

○ Cleaned periodically

○ Monthly test.

### Grade E

○ As Grade D but with no battery back-up.

The exact fire warning system installed 'should take account of the building, the layout, the number and types of occupants, the standard of management applied by the landlords and the condition of the property'[25]. As stated at the beginning of chapter 2, all standards recommended by guidance are advisory. However, in the absence of a clear legal requirement, the standards for fire warning systems set out in the guidance would be relied upon in any court proceedings.

## Installation, maintenance and repair

However good your alarm system is, it must be guaranteed to work in a fire.

Where a Grade A system is installed, an installer must follow BS 5839 and should give an HMO landlord, or person acting for them, a certificate of installation and commissioning and a logbook. The system should be installed so that if there is a fault in one area or a detector is removed, the rest of the system still works.

---

25. Department of the Environment, Transport and the Regions: Letter to local authorities, dated 28 April 1999: Houses in Multiple Occupation: Guidance on Standards

A landlord or manager should appoint a responsible person to supervise and maintain the system and keep proper records. There should be clear procedures for dealing with alarms (i.e. not just switching the system off until an engineer calls). BS 5839 requires a daily check to see that the control panel of a Grade A system indicates normal operation. Additionally, at least one detector should be tested each week. A quarterly inspection should include checking the logbook, any back-up batteries, the alarm sounders, the fault indicators etc. An annual inspection should include testing every detector, visually checking the whole system and going over the quarterly checks. The logbook should contain details of all servicing, alarms, practice drill, defects, disconnection and other incidents. Lastly the electrical wiring should be tested every five years in accordance with British Standard 7671[26].

Local authorities can assist with this checking by asking for a copy of the annual certificate showing the alarm system has been checked by a competent person.

Grade D and E systems should be cleaned periodically as recommended by the manufacturers. The system should be tested each month by operating all alarm sounders in the HMO. This is usually done using the test button on each smoke alarm or by using an approved testing product – not a naked flame. All detectors should be tested once a year to ensure that they respond to smoke.

26. British Standard 7671:1992 Requirements for electrical installations, Institution of Electrical Engineers Wiring Regulations, 16th Edition.

## Section 2: FIRE ESCAPE

At the heart of fire safety is the **protected escape route.** This is a special route which, whilst running through the building, is effectively separated off from all the adjacent rooms by fire resisting materials. The route may comprise of stairs, corridors, walkways or passages but, in the event of a fire, it must allow occupants to escape safely to a final exit.

## Protected escape routes

In order to achieve the above, the protected route must incorporate the following features:

- All floors, ceilings, walls, or partitions (including any glass) must remain **fire resistant** for a specified time, considered adequate to allow all the occupants to escape. This means that there should be no **holes** or **gaps** in the route.

- Almost all doors leading on to the route should be **fire doors,** with smoke seals.

- The route must be wide enough to allow everyone to exit safely. It must be kept clear of obstructions at all times. In particular, no **fire hazards** should be placed in the route. There must be an easy **means of opening** all escape route doors.

- Unless the route is used regularly by occupants and is straightforward, it should be well signposted with **escape notices** so that people can clearly see how to escape the building.

- The route must be well lit, if necessary by adequate **escape lighting.**

- All the **surface finishes** must not allow the easy spread of fire or expel toxic gases.

## Protected lobbies

A protected lobby is any area which acts like a buffer zone to confine the spread of fire, smoke or fumes. This is achieved by the walls, ceilings, floors and doors of the lobby having a similar standard of fire resistance as the rest of the protected escape route. A protected lobby could be an entrance hall, an area outside lifts or part of a corridor. For instance, if a self-contained bedsit has a small entrance hall which has been made into a protected lobby, any fire inside the bedsit would have difficulty penetrating into the lobby and then into other areas of the building. Equally, any fire which starts in other parts of the building would take considerable time to penetrate the lobby and then into the bedsit.

## Secondary protected escape routes

In some buildings, only one protected escape route may not be sufficient and a secondary means of escape may be required. If this is the case, occupants must not have to cross one escape route to reach another. If necessary one escape route should bypass the other by means of balconies, bypass corridors or, in exceptional circumstances, intercommunicating doors between rooms. If balconies are used as an alternative means of escape, they must not be threatened by smoke or flames from openings such as windows. This is far from easy to guarantee in practice. Escape via balconies must not lead to dead ends from where there is no escape route.

## Upwards escape routes

Although most protected escape routes will lead downwards to a final exit on the ground floor, it is also possible to provide an escape route which leads upwards. If an upwards escape route is used, a fire door and fire resisting screen must be installed at the third floor and on alternate floors above (i.e. 5th floor, 7th floor) in a manner which separates the upwards and downward flights of stairs at those levels.

There are two main ways of providing an upwards escape route:

1. A protected escape route to the roof and, from there, a safe route to the ground floor of the premises next door. If the stairway finishes at the top floor landing, a portable ladder is not acceptable to reach the roof. A permanent stairway is needed or 'exceptionally' a ladder which meets a British Standard. Any trapdoor or doorway to the roof must be at least 550mm wide and 800mm high to ensure that all occupants are able to pass through with ease. If a trapdoor is used it should open automatically and remain fully open. Escape routes across flat roofs or through a roof void (i.e. loft), must be on safe, non-skid surfaces. These should normally be at least 800mm wide and have adequate headroom. All walkways should have guard rails at least 1100mm high.

2. A protected escape route to a building next door through the wall separating the two buildings on the top floor. A self-closing fire door must be installed and this could have a panic bolt or latch. It must not have a key or involve breaking glass.

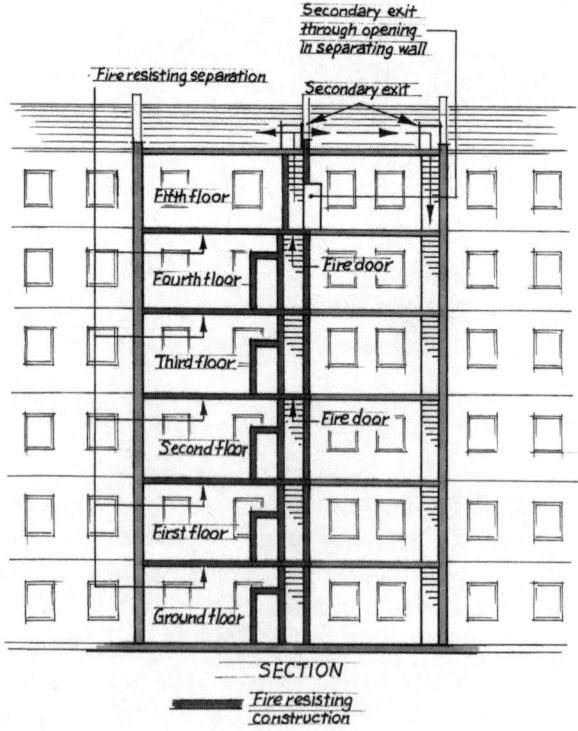

Both of these methods involve using the next-door building. This is frowned on by many fire experts. Escape routes in the next-door building may be blocked or locked. The next-door owners may be worried over security or may have sold the building to someone who knows nothing about this escape route and may even brick it up. Therefore, the use of an alternative escape route within the control of your HMO is usually more satisfactory.

### Escape routes in hostels

The Government HMO guidance states that, in hostels, the only fire doors which can connect directly to a protected escape route are those which lead to:

- toilets with no fire risks

- protected lobbies

- corridors

- final exits

- lift wells.

This means that if a route is connected via single fire doors to other areas (e.g. living accommodation or an office) it would **not** count as a protected escape route, even if it was built entirely from fire resistant materials. Instead, it would be considered as a stairway enclosure. This is a very important distinction, since it affects distances of travel in hostels.

# Fire resistance

### What is fire resistance?

The relevant British Standard[27] specifies that, in order to be resistant to fire, building materials must pass strict standards in three areas:

- **Stability** to withstand a fire without collapse.

- **Integrity** to resist the penetration of fire, smoke and fumes.

- **Insulation** to resist excessive heat penetration (so that the fire does not spread by radiation or conduction through to the other side).

### Fire resistance times

Fire resistance standards are measured in terms of the time, and so construction materials must be resistant to fire for a minimum period of time. The usual minimum periods used in HMOs are 30 minutes and 60 minutes, but longer periods can apply. The Government HMO guidance recommends minimum fire resistance times for various parts of the structure of a building.

---

## Table 1: Recommended minimum fire resistance times (minutes)

| | Walls | Fire Doors | Floors and structural elements |
|---|---|---|---|
| Enclosing:<br>● a protected escape route or lobby<br>● a lift well or stairway<br>● individual occupancies of self-contained dwellings | 30 | 30 | |
| Enclosing an area of higher fire risk | 60 | 60 | |
| Enclosing a stairway to a basement | 60 | 60 (or two 30s) | |
| Above a basement<br>In a house of 3 or more storeys | | | 60 or 30[28] |
| In a 2 storey house | | | 30 |

### Hotels and boarding houses

In hotels and boarding houses, there are different standards for fire resistance times. There should be a minimum 30 minutes fire resistance for all floors, doors and walls, which:

- enclose a protected route

- enclose a stairway

- enclose a lift well or lift motor room

- enclose a compartment.

Where there are higher risk areas, the walls, doors and floors should all have 60 minutes fire resistance.

The main exceptions to these two general rules are:

- corridors that are sub-divided can have 20 minute fire doors

- there must be two 30-minute doors between a basement and a ground floor

- floors over basements should be 60-minute fire resistant.

### Fire resistant materials

Many different materials may be used for constructing a building. There are also many special building boards which can sometimes be used to add to old forms of construction or to replace old materials. Most traditional forms of construction material (e.g. brick, concrete, plasterboard) will pass the above British Standard tests and provide half-hour or modified half-hour fire resistance (i.e. they would be expected to remain stable for 30 minutes and maintain integrity and insulation for 15 minutes). The kind of materials which are far less resistant to fire include partitions made of single sheets of blockboard or plywood; stud partitions with hardboard or some types of fibreboard and untreated timber. The resistance of construction materials will also depend on their thickness.

---

28. In HMOs of 3 or more storeys, the guidance states that 30 minute fire resistance is usually enough, provided an LD2 AFD is provided. Where no such AFD is provided (e.g. in a two storey house with a basement), then 60 minute fire resistance is needed.

## Glass

Glass can be a real danger in a fire, as the everyday type will shatter within a few minutes when exposed to fire or excessive heat, allowing smoke and flames to spread freely. Therefore, to ensure that a protected route is completely fire resistant, any glass along the route must meet the same standards of fire resistance as the other building materials. Examples of glass along a protected route include fan lights above doors, or timber and glass screens separating the escape route from the stairway.

There are three main types of special fire resistant glass:

- uninsulated glass – glass that keeps its integrity (i.e. does not crack, break or allow gases to penetrate)

- insulated or insulating glass – glass that also restricts the temperature rise on the other side of the glass during a fire

- safety glass – glass that performs two functions by resisting fire and protecting against accidents. This is needed in locations where occupants would be injured if the glass was to break (e.g. less than 800mm above floor level in windows or glazed panels, or within 1500mm of the floor in doors).

The fire resistance of glass also depends on its dimensions, the type of frame and how it is secured. TRADA (The Timber Research and Development Association) recommends any timber beading holding the glass in place should cover the edge of the glass by at least 15mm to prevent the glass pulling out under extreme heat. This beading should, in turn be secured to the frame with 30mm steel pins or screws. Many different glazing systems have been produced and tested by manufacturers. Their specifications must be followed exactly, or the glazing may fail. The Glass and Glazing Federation issues a leaflet on glazing safety to prevent the spread of fire and smoke[29].

> Wired glass is used extensively. It will crack early in a fire but be held together by the wire mesh. If the glass is 6mm thick and not over 1.2 m$^2$ in area then half-hour fire resistance can be provided. However the edges of this glass need a good cover strip, otherwise in fire they may pull out of the frame.

## Construction work

Finally, fire resistant materials will only be effective if they have been built to specification. Most traditional forms of construction will give half-hour or modified half-hour fire resistance. However, if the actual construction is not up to standard, the construction materials will do little to resist fire penetration. Examples of poor construction include:

- loose and defective plasterwork to the ceiling

- plain edged or badly fitting tongued and grooved floor boarding

---

29. Copies of this leaflet can be obtained from the Glass and Glazing Federation on 0171 403 7177 at a cost of £5.00 each.

- partitions made of single sheets of blockwood or plywood

- stud partitions with hardboard or some types of fibreboard.

The following example shows how apparently minor changes can make a major difference to fire resistance.

> Take a typical floor to a first storey room. It has 15mm thick tongued and grooved timber floorboards and joists which are at least 38mm wide, with gaps of 400mm between the joists. The ceiling might be 15mm thick and made of laths (little strips of softwood) and plaster. This whole floor could achieve what is called modified half-hour fire resistance. However, if one layer of 15mm thick plasterboard was used on the ceiling, with the joints of the boards taped and filled and backed by the timber joists, then the fire resistance would be half-hour. Finally, if two layers of plasterboard, with joints staggered and external joints taped and filled giving a total thickness of 25mm, were used together with joists as wide as 47mm, then it would achieve a full one-hour fire resistance.

These may appear very technical and minor details. However, they show how the type and thickness of the construction material used, and the way it is constructed, can make a huge difference to the length of time occupants will have to safely escape a fire via the protected route.

## Holes, gaps, cavities and service ducts

Even if a protected route or other parts of a building are built from fire resistant materials, smoke and fumes will still penetrate if there are holes or gaps in the construction. These may exist for a variety of reasons. There may be holes in the walls or ceilings because of disrepair, or there may be gaps around service pipes, wiring or ventilation ducts running from another part of the building. Such gaps must not allow smoke or fumes to penetrate a protected route, or spread to adjoining accommodation, particularly from rooms where there is a high risk of fire (e.g. kitchens).

Therefore, the Government HMO guidance recommends that a detailed inspection of the building should be made to identify any holes or cavities. Where such gaps are found to exist, they should be firestopped. Non-combustible materials (e.g. iron or steel service pipes penetrating a wall, floor or ceiling) can be firestopped with an intumescent paste or similar to prevent fire or smoke spreading. Other combustible materials (e.g. PVC-u, lead or aluminium) should also be firestopped or alternatively they should be fitted with an intumescent collar. They could also be boxed in with fire resisting materials, unless the building has been converted to current Building Regulations and pipes are less than 40mm in diameter.

Many existing HMOs may have pipes and wires boxed in but the duct will often not be fire resistant. There are often small gaps between ceilings and walls or floors and walls. These should be filled, preferably from both sides, with an intumescent sealant (in a similar way to the sealant applied around a bath). Single cables passing through the structure can be sealed in the same way.

# Surface finishes to walls and ceilings

The surface finish to most walls, partitions and ceilings is usually paint or wallpaper but in some cases can be different materials (e.g. tiles, plastic, wood). Surface finishes are very important since they may hinder or help the spread of flames. The rapid spread of flames across surfaces allows the fire to spread more rapidly and so reduces the time for escape. Surfaces must resist the spread of flame and, if ignited, not release heat at an excessive rate.

Government guidance on standards in HMOs[30], and hotels and boarding houses[31] provides examples of acceptable surface finishes. These are based on the fire resistance rating of building materials contained in the current Building Regulations[32]. Examples of acceptable and unacceptable surface finishes are listed below.

## Acceptable surface finishes

The following surface finishes can be used anywhere:

- special fire resisting boards, such as Masterboard and Supalux

- plasterboard and plaster finishes

- brickwork

- blockwood

- concrete

- ceramic tiles

- hardwood with impregnation treatment

- woodwool slab (rarely used now)

- thin wallpapers, if applied to inorganic surfaces such as plaster or brickwork

- flame retardant paints.

Asbestos products were previously included in this category but, for health and safety reasons, they should no longer be used.

## Unacceptable surface finishes

The following surface finishes are not acceptable on protected routes or any ceilings, unless they have been treated with a regularly maintained flame retardant coating to give them the same fire resistance as the above finishes. Where such coatings have been used, a landlord can be asked to provide proof of this. However, non-treated finishes can be used on other walls provided the total area does not exceed 20 square metres or half the floor area (whichever is the smaller):

- timber

- hardboard

---

30. DoE Circular No.12/92, *Houses in Multiple Occupation: Guidance to local housing authorities on standards of fitness under section 352 of the Housing Act 1985*. 31. *DoE Guide to Fire Precautions in Hotels and Boarding Houses*. 32. Approved Document B to the Building Regulations, 1991

- chipboard

- blockboard

- fibre insulating board

- thermosetting plastics or decorative laminates (e.g. melamine, formica)

- thick or flocked wallpapers

- thermoplastics (e.g. polythene, PVC-u sheeting, perspex, polystyrene – often used as wall lining). If used in the acceptable areas mentioned above, they: (a) must not exceed a thickness of 5mm on walls or 12mm on ceilings, (b) must be applied to an inorganic surface and (c) should only be finished with one coat of water-based emulsion (gloss paint should never be used on such surfaces).

## Hazards and obstructions

The Government HMO guidance states that, because they are potential fire hazards, the following items should never be permitted in protected escape routes:

- portable heaters, oil heaters, heaters with unprotected flames or radiant bar fires, or fixed fuel heaters using a gas supply cylinder

- cooking appliances

- upholstered furniture

- wardrobes or other storage furniture

- coat racks

- storage of any kind (unless it is kept in a locked fire-resistant cupboard)

- lighting using naked flames

- gas meters that are not especially protected.

The above list emphasises the need not only to prevent the start of a fire in stairways and corridors but also to keep all escape routes clear of obstructions at all times: in other words, 24 hours a day, 365 days a year. For instance, leaving personal belongings from a cleared flat at the base of the stairs awaiting collection; storing some new kitchen units, polythene wrapped, in a common hallway until someone fits them; or piles of old magazines left on the landing are all totally unacceptable. The Government HMO guidance recommends that notices stating the need to keep escape routes free from obstruction should be placed in key areas (e.g. open spaces beneath stairs).

## Means of opening escape route doors

The Government HMO guidance makes it clear that there should be no method for opening doors used for means of escape that 'involves the use of a key nor should it require the breaking of glass'. This includes the main front entrance door – people have died trying to find their own front door key in a fire. The CIEH (London and Greater Manchester) Guides recommend five-lever internal mortice locks, released with a thumb turn with latch and lever handles, for this purpose. Panic bolts and latches, which can be seen on emergency fire-exit doors in cinemas or other large buildings, allow the door to be opened easily from the inside but not allow anyone to gain access from the outside. The relevant British Standard[33] states that doors with panic bolts should be checked weekly.

Door bolts are difficult to operate in case of fire, whilst roller catches and ball catches are not considered reliable enough to hold a fire-door tightly shut. Other forms of emergency bolts and latches which would not normally be suitable are break glass bolts (where the glass is broken to operate a bolt to open a door) and locking key boxes with glass. These are often used for doors which separate one building from another but it is by no means unknown for the key to be missing.

Apart from the use of panic bolts and latches, all escape route doors used as a means of escape must be kept unlocked at all times.

# Distances of travel

A basic principle of fire safety is to limit the distance anyone has to travel to reach a place of safety. In thick smoke and gases, and with little or no light to help, having to travel too far to escape could cost someone's life.

The distance of travel is the actual distance that occupants must travel between any point in the building, and:

- the nearest final exit from which they can safely leave the vicinity of the building

- the nearest door to a protected escape route.

There are no restrictions on the distance of travel once inside a protected escape route, as this should be safe.

There are standards for maximum travel distances for a variety of situations. They are not meant to be totally hard and fast rules. However, if they are exceeded then the safety of all occupants could be put at risk. Other additional fire safety measures may make up for slightly longer distances of travel.

## All HMOs except hostels, hotels and boarding houses

The following standards apply only to HMOs where the highest floor is not more than 11m above ground level and there is only one single staircase. Where there is more than one staircase or the building is taller, different principles are usually followed and the use of Building Regulations standards may be more appropriate.

Three maximum travel distances are set by Government guidance:

- 9 metres from any point in a living room or bedroom to the room exit

- 9 metres from the exit of any room to the entrance to the accommodation

- 7.5 metres from the entrance to the accommodation to the nearest escape route.

The guidance offers no solution if these limits cannot be met. The *CIEH (Greater Manchester) Guide* recommends some degree of flexibility where the maximum is exceeded but emphasises that other factors affecting the means of escape should be considered.

## Hostel accommodation

Different maximum distances of travel are recommended for hostels. The following apply to hostels where people can be expected to escape from a building unaided when necessary. It assumes minimal staff supervision at night.

> Note: If the hostel provides for disabled people then different standards are likely to apply. This will depend on the height of the building and whether the residents require supervision at night[34].

Table 2 below shows the recommended maximum travel distances If you are within a room and then go to a room exit and to a final exit. There are two sets of figures depending on whether it is possible to escape in one direction or in more than one direction.

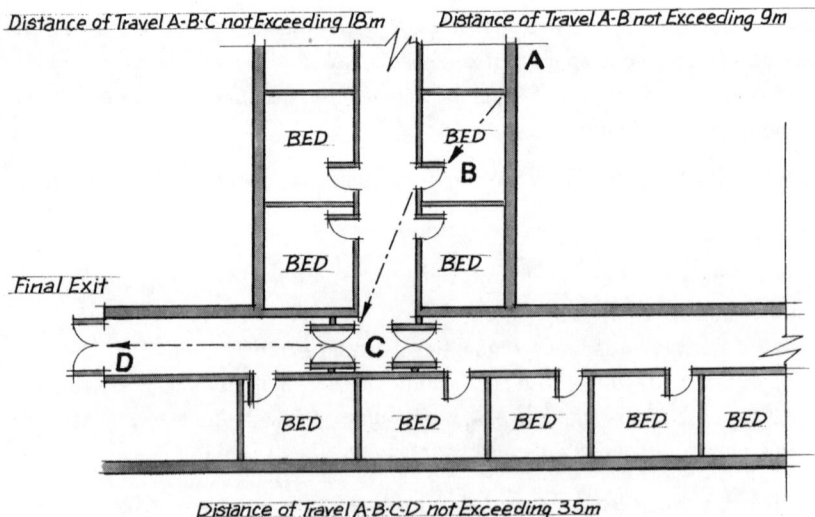

Distance of Travel A-B-C not Exceeding 18m    Distance of Travel A-B not Exceeding 9m

Distance of Travel A-B-C-D not Exceeding 35m

Two escape routes are obviously safer than one, so the minimum travel distances are longer where two escape routes exist.

  34. Health Technical Memorandum or Fire Service Circular 11/1993, as appropriate.

## Table 2: Recommended maximum travel distances in hostels

| | Where escape is possible in more than one direction | | Where escape is possible in one direction only | |
|---|---|---|---|---|
| | To room exit | To final exit | To room exit | To final exit |
| Sleeping areas and all other situations | 18m | 35m | 9m | 18m |
| Area of higher fire risk | 12m | 25m | 6m | 12m |

Sometimes you may have to travel through another room to reach the nearest room exit. This is called an access room, because it gives access to the exit door. The room you started from is called an inner room. In cases where there are inner and access rooms, the maximum travel distances to the nearest exit from the access room are:

- six metres from an inner room used as sleeping accommodation or an area of higher fire risk

- nine metres from an inner room used for any other purpose (e.g. living room).

All exits must be at least 750mm wide but the exact width depends on the number of occupants. The Government HMO guidance also requires more than one exit for any room occupied by more than 30 people. It is important that if there are two or more exits they are not clustered together. Otherwise fire in that area could prevent use of all exits. So a rule, called the 45 degree rule, has been devised. If you draw a line from any point in a room to the exits, the angle between the two lines must not be less than 45 degrees.

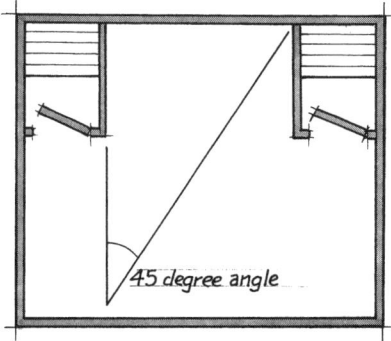

If the angle is less than 45 degrees, it is considered that escape is possible in one direction only and so the maximum travel distances, in the right hand columns of Table 2 above, must on no account be exceeded.

## Hotels and boarding houses
Different travel distances are also recommended for hotels and boarding houses.

The maximum travel distances until you reach:

- a final exit (e.g. main entrance door, fire exit door), or

- a door to a stairway which is a protected route, or

- a door to a protected lobby, or

- a door that is a means of escape in a wall (e.g. to another safe building or area) are shown in Tables 3 and 4 below.

**Table 3: Escape in more than one direction – maximum travel distances:**

| From any point | Within room | Total distance |
|---|---|---|
| Sleeping area | 15m | 32m |
| Area of high fire risk | 12m | 25m |
| All other situations | 18m | 35m |

**Table 4: Escape in one direction only – maximum travel distances:**

| From any point | within room | total distance |
|---|---|---|
| Sleeping area | 8m | 16m |
| Area of high fire risk | 6m | 12m |
| All other situations | 9m | 18m |

# Internal layout

Fires in kitchens and living rooms can develop rapidly, bringing large clouds of smoke and gases. These can invade bedrooms whilst occupants are asleep. Therefore, the internal layout of a dwelling is very important.

Government guidance recommends that, 'where practicable':

- bedrooms are not entered through a living room

- bedroom doors should be nearer an exit from the accommodation than kitchen or living room doors.

The Government also 'strongly recommends' that:

- doors that lead to an inner entrance hall (which leads to the main exit door) should be fitted with flexible seals, should be fire resisting and self-closing.

# Fire doors

## What is a fire door?

For fire safety purposes, the term 'fire door' usually includes the door frame, fixings, heat or smoke seals, self-closing devices and other features. The combination of all these items is commonly referred to as the doorset or door assembly.

Fire doors have two main functions:

- to resist the passage of fire
- to control and limit the spread of smoke and fumes.

The Building Research Establishment emphasises that 'it has erroneously been assumed that a good fire resisting door is also a good smoke control door'[35].

### Fire resistance

Like other fire resistant materials, doors have a specified fire resistance time (e.g. 30 or 60 minutes). Since 1985, fire resistant doors have been classified by their integrity (i.e. how long they resist the penetration of fire). Therefore, if a door is referred to as an FD30, it will be a Fire Door which can resist the penetration of fire for 30 minutes. The letter S, as in FD30S, shows the door is suitable for smoke control.

Another term sometimes still used is a firecheck door. This was based on an old British Standard. It is now an obsolete term but is sometimes still used. The standard of firecheck doors is below that of fire resisting doors. They have less resistance to the passage of hot gases and flames through gaps.

Fire resistant doors must be fitted to all protected escape routes and protected lobbies, and should also be fitted to areas with a high fire risk (e.g. kitchens). They allow occupants to safely escape the building as well as protecting the contents and structure of the building by limiting the spread of fire. Fire doors used as a means of escape should normally open in the direction of escape. Government guidance states that this is compulsory if more than 50 people have to escape.

### Smoke control

Smoke control doors play an important role in the early stages of fire development by preventing smoke logging, for instance in corridors or on stairs. They may also play a useful role in protecting escape routes some distance from the fire. Smoke control doors do not always have to meet fire resistance standards but they should be of substantial construction. They should have good quality smoke seals and self-closers.

> A traditional timber door with thinner timber panels, or cheap, modern flush panel doors (with plywood or hardboard on either side and a cellular core inside), are most definitely not fire doors. In actual fires some have been found to fail within five minutes.

35. Malhotra, H. (1987) *Fire Safety in Buildings*, Building Research Establishment, Watford

The British Standard[36] which defines quality standards for fire doors states that they should have adequate fire resistance, the correct ironmongery, intumescent seals and also smoke seals where necessary. However, this standard has not been widely put into practice and many enforcement officers will only require fire resistance, self closers and a timber rebate to the door frame.

## Other features of fire doors

The wrong type of ironmongery, or items which are ill-fitting, can seriously undermine the effectiveness of any fire door. It is therefore essential that all ironmongery and door furniture is correctly fitted and kept in good repair.

### Self-closers and hinges

Government guidance states that all fire doors (except to cupboards and lift wells) should be fitted with self-closing devices capable of closing the door against any latch. A common defect of self-closers is for the device to pull the door up to the frame but be unable to pull the door shut against the resistance of the latch tongue. The most preferable type of self-closer is a good quality device fixed to the top of the door and the door frame. Devices fitted to the side of the door and frame are often immobilised, damaged or fail to pull the door tightly shut. Parts of the door or frame must never be 'hacked out' to fit self closers.

Although Building Regulations permit the use of rising butt hinges as self closers, there is a very strong case never to use them.

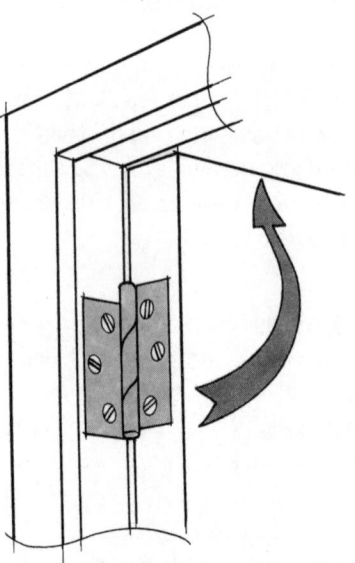

Rising butt hinges are special door hinges, which make the door close on its own.

For such hinges to work there must be a gap of over 4mm between the top of the door and frame when closed. This will undermine the effectiveness of the smoke seal at the very point where, in the event of fire, the most smoke pressure will be present. The *CIEH (London) Guide* points out that two British Standards show that rising butt

36. British Standard 8214:1990: *Code of Practice for Fire Door Assemblies with Non-metallic Leaves*

hinges are unable to act effectively as self-closers. Both the Building Regulations and the Government guidance demand that the hinges must not be combustible and must not melt under 800 degrees centigrade. Screws should also be non-combustible at 800 degrees. Three hinges (sometimes called one and a half pairs) are also needed.

Government guidance and Building Regulations demand that no method should be provided for holding a self-closing fire door in an open position. There are a very few exceptions. The only automatic door release which the Government guidance approves of is one which closes the door when the fire alarm system is set off. Moreover the alarm system must be linked to an automatic fire detector with manual call points. The guidance states that this automatic release should only be fitted when the door cannot be kept closed due to problems in running the premises. However, it should never be fitted to a stairway enclosure and the doors must always be kept shut at night.

### Locks, latches, bolts and handles
Locks and latch tongues should project into the latch plate at least 10mm to allow for any bowing of a fire door in a fire; otherwise it could simply spring open.

### Letterboxes
Requirements for the delivery of mail must never undermine the function of fire doors. The *CIEH (London) Guide* discourages the use of letter plates. The Government HMO Guidance recommends smoke seals to any hinged flap whilst the *CIEH (London) Guide* discourages their insertion but says that certain door assemblies can satisfactorily accommodate them when fitted in the factory.

### Door seals
Fire doors need to be fitted with heat expanding intumescent sealing strips. These expand when the temperature reaches 140 degrees centigrade and effectively seal the gap between the door and its frame.

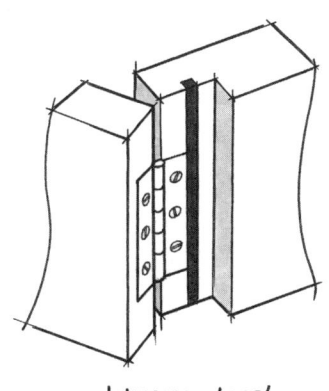

The seal is attached to the top and sides of the door or frame but not the bottom.

*Intumescent seal*

A 30 minute seal is usually 10mm wide whilst a 60-minute seal will be 20mm wide or consist of two 10mm wide strips. Usually the strip is set in a groove in the door edge or in the rebate to the door frame. Unfortunately this exposes it to wear and tear and to being pulled out of place. The strip can also interfere with fitting or adjusting the door. Some manufacturers conceal the strip just below the edges of the door and the rebate to the frame.

For many years a 25mm stop or rebate was seen as a standard requirement for fire doors, unless the frame offered a similar amount of protection.

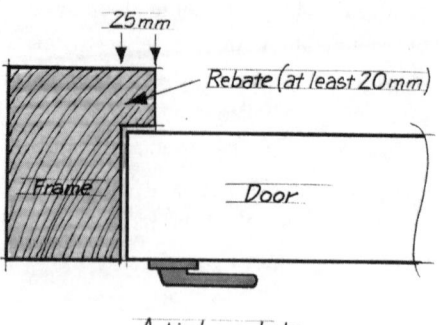

A timber rebate

A stop is a small piece of extra timber attached to the door frame. Its main purpose was considered to be for smoke control. This requirement is based on an obsolete British Standard. However, stops do still have one useful purpose: where there is no rebate to a door frame, they will stop the door swinging too far when it shuts and loosening the hinges. The latest British Standard says this stop is not necessary; however rebates, securely fixed to the frame, are still specified by some local authorities.

One British Standard states that intumescent seals should not be relied on for smoke control as they operate between 140-300 degrees centigrade 'which is too late for the protection of escape routes'. Likewise, rebates in door frames should not be relied on for smoke control 'as in practice doors are likely to warp'. Instead, flexible edge seals are recommended. These are attached to the sides and top of the door or frame. They can be brush seals or bubble seals. They should not be painted over since this will reduce the effectiveness on most seals. The Timber Research and Development Association (TRADA) agrees with this approach in their technical guides[37].

> No room should be tightly sealed where there is a need for fresh air for a room heater such as an open coal fire. However, ventilation should not be provided through the fire doors or by leaving off any seals to a fire door.

### Door frames
A further key factor in smoke control is the fit of the door to the frame. Gaps between either the door edge and the frame or between the face of the door and the stop, will assist the passage of smoke or flames. If the existing frame does not meet the standard required, it must be replaced.

 37. TRADA (1990) *Technology of fire resisting doorsets and* (1988) *Fire resisting door leaflets*

It is also important that there is no gap between the frame and the surrounding wall. This is a dangerous weak spot, often neglected and hidden by a piece of architrave. If this is the case, the architrave should be removed and the gap should be filled with a suitable material (e.g. cement mortar, gypsum plaster, certain glass rock fibres or an intumescent mastic).

Gaps should be no larger than 4mm between the door and the frame when it is closed. Any smoke seal is ignored when considering this gap. Gaps of less than 3mm may make it difficult to close the door with a self-closer.

The *CIEH (London) Guide* recommends a gap of no more than 8mm beneath the door. Large gaps at the bottom of the door do not usually cause integrity failure as cold air is being drawn towards the fire. However, in larger buildings doors remote from the fire may allow cold smoke to pass under the doors.

### Making existing doors into fire doors

In theory, an existing door can be upgraded to become a fire door by the addition of sheet insulation material, intumescent coats or even splitting it in half and inserting a fire resisting core[38]. However, the labour cost and the chance of not achieving a satisfactory door, make it preferable to install new fire doorsets. Many fire brigades no longer consider upgrading a satisfactory solution and insist on a completely new doorset.

### How to identify a fire door

Many manufacturers make doors with different materials. Whilst internal linings may be chipboard, flaxboard, cork, timber or a mineral core, external surfaces might be hardboard or plywood. For this reason, it is often difficult to tell a fire door from a normal mass-manufactured door. A guide used to be the weight and thickness of the door (e.g. a 44mm door would be half-hour whilst a 54mm was a full hour). However, you can now get 44mm doors with three hour fire resistance. Professionals involved in fire safety develop a special 'nose' for doors by using their senses – looking for heavier doors, listening for a solid sound when tapped and using their eyes to pick up clues concerning the materials used. For anyone else, recognising older fire doors is not always easy.

Fortunately, for many years now a colour code has been used on the edge of new fire doors. This code is on the edge where the hinges are fixed. The colour code will also indicate whether a special intumescent strip has been used.

---

38. TRADA (01494 563091) publishes a range of short technical notes on fire doors and how glazing should be fixed for fire safety purposes

**Table 6: Range of colour codes for fire doors giving method of performance identification for non-metallic doors and frames.**

| Core Colour | Background | Integrity (minutes) | Colour Code Interpretation |
|---|---|---|---|
| Red | White | 20 | |
| | Yellow | 30 | Intumescent seals require to be fitted at |
| | Pink | 45 | time of original installation. |
| | Blue | 60 | |
| Green | White | 20 | |
| | Yellow | 30 | No additional intumescent seal need be |
| | Pink | 45 | fitted at time of installation. |
| | Blue | 60 | |
| Blue* | White | 20 | With no intumescent seal fitted. |
| | White | 30 | With intumescent seal fitted in either door edge or frame. |

*Only door constructions with a fire resistance rating of 30 minutes that satisfy both FD20 without an additional intumescent seal fitted and FD30 with an intumescent seal fitted are marked with a blue/white plug.

In addition, each new type of fire door should have been tested by a United Kingdom Accreditation Service (UKAS) registered test centre and have a manufacturer's test report. This will also set out requirements for the frame and its fitting as well as acceptable ironmongery.

If fire doors have been altered, the *CIEH (London) Guide* recommends there should be an assessment report or a 'field of application report' by a suitably qualified engineer.

## Escape lighting

To ensure that a protected escape route can be safely and effectively used at all times, it must be well lit. This means that the normal lighting on escape routes should be in good order and provide safe illumination. It also means that emergency lighting may be necessary in case the power supply to the normal lighting fails during the fire.

British Standard 5266[39] states that there are three main aims of escape lighting:

1 To help indicate clearly the escape routes.

2 To allow safe movement towards and through exits.

3 To ensure fire alarm call points and fire fighting equipment can be readily located.

In order to meet these aims, the British Standard states that.

- Escape lighting should be positioned so that anyone in any part of the building is clear as to what escape route to follow. This means that all signs marking the exits, emergency exits and escape routes should be illuminated.

- Escape lighting should also be positioned at other key points. Such points may include changes in direction and the intersection of corridors; near fire alarm call points and fire-fighting equipment; near each staircase and exit door.

39. British Standard 5266:Part 1:1988.

- There should be regular testing of escape lighting at monthly and six-monthly intervals. There should be a further test three years after installation and each year thereafter. A log of these tests should be kept on the premises 'in the care of a responsible person'.

## Standards for normal lighting

The Government HMO guidance states that normal lighting should allow people to move around safely at night.

If the normal lighting system is operated by time switches, these should allow plenty of time before the lighting is cut off. The *CIEH (London) Guide* recommends four minutes.

## Standards for emergency lighting

The Government HMO guidance sets no clear standards for emergency lighting but states that it may be necessary, depending on individual circumstances and the complexity of the layout of the building.

BS5266 states that emergency lighting should activate within 15 seconds (preferably within five seconds where people are unfamiliar with the building) of the failure of normal lighting supply. The emergency lighting system should operate for a minimum of one hour. Vehicle batteries are not normally suitable for backing up the power supply to normal lighting.

# Escape notices

There are no specific regulations stating when and where notices are required. However the Government HMO guidance makes recommendations for the use of notices on fire doors and in escape routes. Consequently, most EHOs will require the recommendations as a standard in HMOs.

The design and content of fire safety signs and notices is covered by a British Standard[40]. In addition, the *CIEH (London) Guide* recommends that the design and content of signs and notices should be in line with the Health and Safety (Safety Signs and Signals) Regulations 1996[41]. Typical signs needed include:

### Fire exit

Any exit which is not normally used should have a Fire Exit notice. This should be placed above the exit or, if this is not possible, wherever it is most likely to be seen and least likely to be obstructed. If, at any point along the escape route, the exit is not clearly visible, or there may be confusion about which direction to follow, there should be further Fire Exit signs. Such signs should have a green background with white symbols, including a directional arrow clearly indicating the way out and a pictogram of a running person (the words Fire Exit are no longer required but are optional). They should be of a size which complies with the relevant British Standard and be sited 2.0-2.5 metres from floor level.

---

40. British Standard 5499: Part 1: 1990. 41. Statutory Instrument 1996/341. These Regulations apply to public buildings, workplaces etc. and not specifically to HMOs. However, for reasons of consistency, the CIEH (London) Guide recommends their use in HMOs.

### Fire Door Keep Shut

Where there is a fire door, unless it is the door to an individual bedsit, flat, boiler room or storeroom, this notice should be displayed at eye level on both sides of the door. The signs should have a blue background with white lettering.

### Fire Escape Keep Clear

This notice should be displayed at eye level on both sides of any door provided solely for a means of escape (e.g. doors connecting to an external fire escape or leading to the building next door). They should also have a blue background with white lettering.

### Fire Door Keep Locked

This sign should be displayed on the outside of any fire door to a cupboard. Again, it should have a blue background with white lettering.

### Push Bar to Open

This should be clearly displayed on any door with a panic bolt or latch. It should have a green background with white lettering

---

**Smoke seals and properly maintained alarm and lighting systems can save lives**

In 1994, a 20 month old child and a 33 year old woman died in a fire in an HMO in Scarborough. The coroner's inquest found that this hotel, which consisted of five terraced houses with three floors and a basement, had been substantially altered over time. However, the local housing authority and the local fire authority had not been informed of many of these alterations.

The hotel had a fire certificate and contained fire doors, some smoke and heat detectors, a fire alarm system and escape lighting. Over a period it changed from being a tourist hotel to an HMO providing accommodation for otherwise homeless people, including children.

When a fire broke out, one woman and two children were trapped in smoke-logged rooms on the second floor. One child was rescued successfully, but the other died from the 'inhalation of smoke gases'. There were no smoke seals on their doors.

Subsequent investigations of the alarm and escape lighting systems uncovered a chapter of faults including three separate systems, missing fault indicator bulbs, no maintenance records, missing batteries, missing emergency light bulbs and alarm sounders not working properly.

This tragic incident underlines the need for professionally provided alarm and emergency lighting systems which are kept repaired and well-maintained as well as smoke seals to all fire doors.

# Section 3: FIRE FIGHTING

In many cases, fire-fighting equipment can stop a minor fire developing into a major disaster. However, to be effective, there must be sufficient equipment, well located and in good condition. Moreover equipment must be of the right type and occupants must know how to use them correctly.

> Whilst fire-fighting equipment can prevent the spread of fire, inexperienced users can find it difficult to handle. It is usually more important to get everyone out of the building and telephone the fire brigade, than to attempt to fight a fire.

## Fire extinguishers

The type of fire extinguisher provided and used is very important. This is because extinguishers contain different substances for extinguishing different types of fire. Fire extinguishers will usually contain one of the following:

- water

- carbon dioxide.

Water is suitable for fires of everyday items like wood and paper. However, it can endanger anyone who uses it on electrical fires.

### How to identify types of fire extinguisher

New fire extinguishers are now coded according to their purpose. They are all now red in colour, but also have a coloured panel, which indicates the contents. This panel also has a number and a letter. The letter stands for the type of fire that they will deal with. For instance, a Class A fire involves solid materials, whilst a Class B fire involves liquids (e.g. chip pan fires) and electricity. The two types of extinguisher that will be expected in HMOs are called 13A and 34B:

- 13A is a water type used for general fires

- 34B is a carbon dioxide type used for electrical fires

However, older types of extinguisher, in different colours, will continue to exist for a number of years. These must be checked annually.

### Standards for fire extinguishers

The actual extinguishers should meet the requirements of the relevant British Standards[42].

British Standard 5306[43] specifies the best siting and installation of extinguishers. It states that extinguishers should be sited as close as possible to any fire risk. They should be in conspicuous positions (and certainly not concealed) where they will be readily seen by anyone following an escape route. However they must not cause an obstruction. Positions near to room exits, corridors, stairways, lobbies and landings

---

42. British Standard EN 2:1992; British Standard EN 3 Parts 1-6:1996; British Standard 7863:1996; British Standard 6575:1985; British Standard 5306:Part 3:1985. 43. British Standard 5306: Part 3: 1985.

are the most suitable. No one should have to travel more than 30 metres to an extinguisher. Heavy extinguishers should be 1 metre from the floor and lighter ones 1.5 metres from the floor.

The Government HMO guidance recommends a standard number of extinguishers, depending on the size of the building:

- one 13A extinguisher on each floor up to an area of 100 m$^2$
- two 13 A extinguishers where the floor area is between 100-200 m$^2$
- if the floor area is greater than 200 m$^2$, then there should be two 13As plus one additional 13A for each 200 m$^2$ additional floor area.

The guidance also recommends 'other extinguishing equipment for special risk and fire blankets for communal kitchens'.

British Standard 5306 also recommends an inspection 'not less than quarterly and preferably at least monthly' to check their correct positioning, to check for damage, and to check that they have not been discharged. They should also be serviced annually and inspected by a 'competent' person (e.g. someone with necessary training and experience). This inspection should be recorded on a durable, firmly-fixed label attached to the extinguisher.

## Fire blankets

Fire blankets are generally recommended as the best means of dealing with chip pan or frying pan fires. The Government HMO guidance recommends fire blankets in all shared kitchens in all HMOs.

## Fire sprinkler systems

Although there is currently no legal requirement for the fitting of fire sprinkler systems in residential properties, there is increasing pressure for them to be fitted for life safety purposes. Experience around the world has shown that sprinkler systems can virtually eliminate fire deaths, and reduce injuries and property damage by at least 80%[44]. Sprinklers are of particular benefit in multi-storey buildings (where escape routes may involve many flights of stairs) because they drastically limit the production of smoke and toxic fumes.

Fire sprinkler systems respond automatically to growing fires. They are designed to prevent flashover (see page 6), and control fires before they develop to the point where lives are in danger or serious damage can occur. They are made up of a network of concealed pipes, supplying water to sprinkler heads located at strategic positions within the building and its associated alarm system. Sprinkler systems should protect all habitable spaces and at least one escape route. Each sprinkler head contains a heat-sensitive device, which activates the sprinkler when the temperature reaches a certain level (usually 68°C). The flow of water in the system then triggers the alarm sounders. The sprinkler heads are designed to fit in with residential décors and concealed types are also available.

   44. *Automatic Sprinklers: a 10 year report*, Jim Ford, Chief Fire Officer, Scottsdale, Arizona, USA.

Only qualified and certified engineers should undertake the design and installation of fire sprinkler systems. Once installed, the system should be maintained, and the alarm tested, at least once a year. Sprinkler heads should not be painted, obstructed or used to hang things from. General information on the use of fire sprinklers is contained in BS5306 Part 2, and it is expected that the British Standards Institution will issue a standard for the *Design, Installation and Maintenance of Residential Sprinkler Systems* towards the end of 1999. Other standards available are the *Loss Prevention Council Technical Bulletin TB14* or, more importantly, *US Standards NFPA 13D* and *13R*.

# 4 What to do if standards are not met (1)

## Advice for occupants and their advisers

If you have checked the standards in your accommodation and believe that they fail to meet the required standards, there are a number of options available to you.

The action you decide to take will depend on how serious a risk from fire you are facing. For example, if you feel you are in immediate danger, then you may need to seek professional advice straight away. However, in most cases, it is preferable to start by dealing amicably with the landlord, who may bring the property up to standard without you having to take further action.

## Check your legal rights to occupy the property

It is possible that if you ask for fire safety work to be carried out, the landlord may ask you to leave in order to avoid doing the work. This is why it is important that you check your security of tenure (your legal right to remain living in your home, even if the landlord wants you to leave). The level of security you have will vary depending on your tenure status (e.g. lodger, assured shorthold tenant, protected tenant). The easiest way to clarify your security is to check your tenancy agreement. If you don't have a tenancy agreement, or you are unsure of your rights, you should seek housing advice[45].

## Speak to other occupants

If other people live in your building, speak to them about your worries. You may find that they are just as concerned as you. Together, you will have more chance of success and, if you take action as a group, there will be less risk of any individual being harassed by the landlord.

## Approach your landlord

Tell the landlord about your worries in a letter, asking for a response within a reasonable period (e.g. two weeks). Try to get all occupants to sign the letter and make sure that you keep a copy. If the landlord telephones or calls at the property in response to the letter, make a note of the date and what your landlord said. All landlords have a common law duty of care to ensure that occupants are safe.

45. See Appendix B.

> *If the landlord does not respond to your letter, does not give you a satisfactory response, or fails to take action, you do not necessarily have to take legal action yourself*

## Contact your local council

The local council's Environmental Health Department has a responsibility to enforce fire safety standards, particularly in HMOs. Explain your worries and arrange for an Environmental Health Officer (EHO) to inspect your home. It is best to involve your landlord in this visit. However, if you do not want your landlord to know that you have contacted the council, you can ask the EHO to keep this confidential by carrying out a routine inspection. The main piece of legislation available to EHOs to enforce fire safety standards in HMOs is the Housing Act 1985.

## Housing Act 1985

This is a powerful law allowing local authorities to enforce certain standards in HMOs.

Section 352 of the Act gives EHOs the legal power to demand that all HMOs are suitable for the number of existing occupants by meeting a five-point fitness standard. This includes:

- adequate means of escape from fire

- adequate other fire precautions.

The Government HMO guidance[46] mentioned in chapters 2 and 3 provides local authorities with details of the standards they might expect to be met when exercising this enforcement power. Because this power to take action is discretionary, it means that EHOs are not legally required to enforce fire safety standards in all HMOs in their areas, although in most cases they will do so.

In the case of some higher risk HMOs, EHOs have a legal duty to (i.e. they must) use their enforcement powers to secure improvements to sub-standard fire safety precautions. This mandatory duty is set down in Section 365 of the Act and the properties to which it applies are listed in a Government Order[47]. From 30 September 1999, they include most HMOs of three storeys or more (except those where the accommodation consists entirely of self-contained flats). Any storey which lies wholly or mainly below the floor level of the principal entrance to the house (e.g. some basements) is excluded. Houses of three storeys or more consisting entirely of self-contained flats are included under this duty from 29 February 2000.

In cases where the local authority has a duty to act, or in certain other types of HMO (e.g. care homes), the EHO must consult with the fire authority before taking any enforcement action.

If an HMO does not comply with the fire safety standards, EHOs enforce standards by first serving a preliminary notice (commonly known as a 'minded to' notice) on the

---

46. Department of the Environment Circular 12/92, *Houses in Multiple Occupation: Guidance to local housing authorities on standards of fitness under section 352 of the Housing Act 1985*, plus Department of the Environment, Transport and the Regions: Letter to local authorities, dated 28 April 1999, *Houses in Multiple Occupation: Guidance on Standards*. 47. Housing (Fire Safety in Houses in Multiple Occupation) Order 1997 (S.I. 1997 No.230).

person in control of, or the person managing, the property. This acts as a warning that the council intends to serve a statutory notice as the first step in legal proceedings, and gives the landlord the opportunity to negotiate with the council. However, in cases where the local authority considers there is a need to take immediate enforcement action (such as serious fire risks) the serving of a preliminary notice is not required.

The EHO will then serve a statutory notice (commonly known as a works notice or section 352 notice) on the person in control of, or the person managing, the property, specifying the works required to make the property suitable. The notice must specify the time limits by which the works should start (no earlier than 21 days) and be completed. The local authority must notify all occupants when the notice is served and keep a register of these notices available to the public free of charge. Copies must also be provided on request for a reasonable fee.

## Direction Orders

In addition to, or instead of, requiring works to bring the fire precautions up to standard, sections 354-5 of the Act give EHOs the power to limit the number of occupants who can safely live in the building in its current condition. If such a direction is issued, the number of people currently living in the building must not increase, unless it is within the limit set. This does not mean that any occupants have to leave. Instead, as occupants move out of their own accord, they must not be replaced. This process is known as 'natural wastage' and must continue until the number of occupants is below the limit set. The service of a section 354 notice does not affect the terms of your tenancy agreement. If you are asked to leave by your landlord because a Direction Order has been issued, you should not agree to do so and should obtain housing advice[48].

## Closing Orders

Section 365 & 368 of the Act give EHOs an alternative power to deal with inadequate means of escape from fire. If they believe that the means of escape would be adequate if part of the house (e.g. an attic room) is not used, they can either accept an undertaking from the landlord or issue a Closing Order to ensure that such areas are closed off from human habitation.

## Housing (Management of HMOs) Regulations 1990

Section 369 of the Act gives local authorities the power to take action against the manager of an HMO for failing to observe regulations on proper standards of management. In 1990, the Government issued the Housing (Management of HMOs) Regulations[49], which require HMO managers to ensure the repair, maintenance, cleansing and good order of existing facilities. It is an offence to fail to comply with these regulations. Regulation 10 relates to the means of escape from fire. This requires HMO managers to:

- ensure that all means of escape in the house and all apparatus, systems and other fire precautions are kept in good order and repair, and free from obstruction

48. See Appendix B. 49. Statutory Instrument 1990 No.830.

- ensure signs indicating means of escape are displayed in a visible place.

Regulation 16 places a duty on residents to ensure that the manager can carry out the requirements. Residents must not hinder or frustrate arrangements made by the manager for means of escape and anything provided by way of fire precautions. For example, if fire doors are provided, residents must ensure they are kept closed and that nothing is left in the escape route.

If an HMO does not comply with the Management Regulations on means of escape from fire, an EHO can enforce the Regulations in the same way as enforcement of the fitness standard under section 352. First, a preliminary notice must be served on the manager. This is followed by a statutory notice (commonly known as a section 372 notice) specifying the action needed to put right the neglect in management. This notice must specify the time limits by which the works should start (no earlier than 21 days) and be completed.

## Failure to comply with works notices

Failure to comply with a statutory notice (either under section 352 or section 372 of the Act) is a criminal offence. The local authority can prosecute, or carry out the works themselves in default, or both. If a prosecution is successful, the landlord or manager can be fined. In the case of section 372 offences, fines can be up to £5,000 for each count of non-compliance. Further prosecutions, resulting in further fines, can be brought until the required works are completed.

## Control Orders

Section 379 of the Act gives local authorities the power to enter and take control of an HMO if they feel the living conditions are so bad that quick intervention is necessary to protect the safety, welfare or health of the occupants. This is the most drastic power available to a local authority. Once a control order is in force, the local authority must take any action necessary to bring the house up to a satisfactory standard.

## Fitness for human habitation

Section 604 of the Act requires all houses to meet a general nine-point standard of fitness for human habitation. The requirements of this standard are set out in detail in Government guidance[50]. The standard can cover items of disrepair which might threaten fire safety, such as faulty electrics, broken stairs and missing plaster. If a property fails to meet the section 604 standard, the local authority is responsible for deciding on the most appropriate course of action.

Although the Housing Act 1985 is the main piece of legislation available to EHOs to enforce fire safety standards, other public health legislation is available to them. In some cases, the local authority may decide to take action under other legislation because it will provide a speedier and more effective means of ensuring fire safety, or because there are higher penalties for non-compliance.

50. Department of the Environment Circular No.17/96, *Private Sector Renewal: a Strategic Approach.*

# Environmental Protection Act 1990

Section 79 of this Act states that any premises that are in such a state as to be prejudicial to health or a nuisance are considered a statutory nuisance. Prejudicial to health means it does, or is likely to, cause injury to your health. This could include defects which affect fire safety, such as dangerous electrical wiring, or blocked escape routes. Local authorities have a duty to inspect their areas from time to time to detect statutory nuisance, and to take reasonable steps to investigate complaints of such nuisance.

Section 80 of the Act states that, where the local authority is satisfied that a statutory nuisance exists, the EHO has a duty to serve an abatement notice. This can be served on either the person responsible for the nuisance or the owner of the property. The notice can require the nuisance to stop or be rectified within specified time limits. Such notices can require action within a day if the situation is very urgent and such a time-scale can be seen as reasonable.

If the person responsible for the nuisance fails to comply with the notice, a criminal offence has been committed. This means that the local authority can prosecute. Those found guilty of such an offence can be liable for a fine of up to £5,000.

Although this Act has been used in the past to ensure against risks to fire safety, the expressions 'prejudicial' or 'injurious' to health remain open to debate. An important case in 1998[51] has cast doubt about the application of the Act to some fire safety risks. In this case, the judge ruled that a steep and narrow staircase, which the tenant felt increased the risk of an accident, did not constitute a statutory nuisance. It was the judge's view that the purpose of the Act was not to protect against the danger of accidental injury, but to cover concerns about the risk of disease or illness. As a result, EHOs may be reluctant to use section 79 of the Act for fire safety enforcement purposes.

# Building Act 1984

If a local authority believes that using the procedures under section 80 of the Environmental Protection Act (i.e. an abatement notice) would cause an unreasonable delay in remedying a defective property, Section 76 of the Building Act 1984 can be used instead. This gives local authorities the power to carry out the work themselves, and recover the cost of this from the owner. In order to take this action, a notice must be served on the owner or person causing the nuisance, giving them nine days to start to put right the defects. After nine days have expired, the local authority has the power to carry out the works in default.

Section 72 of the Building Act applies to certain buildings (including flats, tenements and boarding houses), which are more than two storeys high and where the upper storey is more than 20 feet above the ground. It places a duty on local authorities to require that the owners of, or those proposing to erect, such buildings provide the necessary means of escape from fire. It is up to the local authority, after

---

51. R versus Bristol City Council ex parte Sandra Everett (Queen's Bench Division), 12 March 1998.

consultation with the local fire authority, to decide what is necessary.

In order to carry out its duty under section 72, section 99 of the Act requires the local authority to serve a notice on the owner of the building, indicating the nature of the works required and the time limit within which they must be carried out. Failure to comply with such a notice is a criminal offence. The local authority can prosecute, or carry out the works themselves in default, or both. If a prosecution is successful, the landlord or manager can be fined up to £2,500 for non-compliance.

## Building Regulations 1991

Section 1 of the Building Act 1984 gives the Government the power to make regulations with respect to the design and construction of (and provision of services, fittings and equipment in) buildings of all types. These are known as the Building Regulations. In 1991, the Government issued the latest Building Regulations[52] and these were last amended in 1994. The Government also issues a series of Approved Documents, containing practical guidance on how the requirements of the Building Regulations can be met. Approved Document B[53] provides guidance on fire safety requirements.

One of the main aims of the Building Regulations is to secure the health, safety, welfare and convenience of people who may, in any way, be affected by buildings. This includes fire safety. The regulations apply to all new buildings[54]. They also apply where there has been a significant change to the use, or structure, of an existing building (e.g. house converted into flats). If something is being repaired or replaced, the regulations would not normally apply.

The Building Regulations are interpreted and enforced by Building Control Officers (BCO), who are normally based in the Planning Department or Building Control Department of the local authority. The plans for any intended work to which the regulations apply must be submitted to a BCO for approval. The regulations also require that building work should be carried out with proper materials and in a workmanlike manner.

Building work, and particularly conversion work, carried out without Building Regulations approval could pose a serious fire risk. If an owner does not seek approval, or carries out work which contravenes the Building Regulations, then Section 36 of the Building Act 1984 gives BCOs the power to serve a notice, requiring the work to be brought into compliance (or, in some cases, removed). Such a notice must be served within 12 months of the completion of the work. If the owner fails to comply with the notice, the local authority can carry out the required works and recover the cost from the owner. The local authority can also take action in a Magistrates Court for contravention of the regulations. The penalty on conviction is a fine of up to £5,000.

If you feel that recent works to your dwelling fall within the scope of the Building Regulations, but may not be up to the standards for fire safety, you should contact the local authority Building Control Officers.

52. Statutory Instrument 1991/2786. 53. Department of the Environment, Transport and the Regions, 1992, *The Building Regulations 1991: Fire Safety: Approved Document B.* 54. The current Building Regulations (1991) came into force on 1 June 1992.

# Health and Safety at Work Act 1974

Section 3(2) of this Act places a duty on all self-employed people to conduct their undertakings in such as way as to ensure that other people are not exposed to risks to their health and safety. This legislation has been used successfully against private landlords who have put the health and safety of residents at risk. However, in most cases where there is a risk to fire safety, other legislation is usually more applicable.

Local authorities are responsible for enforcing the Act in premises where the main activity is the provision of privately rented residential accommodation. In premises used for a combination of accommodation and other activities, where there is a higher risk of fire, the Health and Safety Executive[55] may become involved.

It is a criminal offence to fail to discharge a duty under section 3 of the Act. This means that the enforcing authority can bring a prosecution in a Magistrates Court.

# Consumer Protection Act 1987

Section 10 of this Act[56] places a duty on those who supply any consumer goods to ensure that they comply with general safety requirements. The Trading Standards Department at your local council has a duty to enforce these requirements. Section 11 of the Act allows the Government to issue regulations giving details of the requirements to be met by particular goods.

### Furniture and Furnishings (Fire) (Safety) Regulations 1988 (as amended in 1989 and 1993)

These Regulations were issued by the Government under the 1987 Act. They place a duty on any person who supplies items of furniture and furnishings in the course of business to ensure that the items comply with fire resistance requirements. This includes landlords, letting agents or estate agents whose businesses involve the supply of such items as part of a residential furnished letting. It is not intended to apply to people who let their own homes on a short-term, one-off basis (e.g. whilst they are working away), as this is not seen as a business. Landlords who fail to comply with the regulations also run the risk of invalidating their buildings insurance policies.

The Regulations apply to domestic furniture which contains any amount of filling material (e.g. foam). This includes the following:

- domestic upholstered furniture (e.g. beds, sofa beds and children's furniture)

- nursery furniture containing upholstery

- garden furniture containing upholstery

- scatter cushions and seat pads

- pillows

55. The Health and Safety Executive can be contacted on 0541 545500. 56. This section has now largely been replaced by the General Product Safety Regulations 1994, although this does not affect the 1988 Regulations.

- secondary covers for upholstered furniture (e.g. loose covers and stretch covers).

The Regulations do not apply to furniture made before 1950, or re-upholstered furniture made before that date.

The fire resistance requirements of the Regulations are as follows:

- upholstered articles must have fire resistant filling material (e.g. any polyurethane foam filling must be of the 'safer combustion modified foam')
- most cover fabrics must have passed a match resistance test
- the combination of the cover fabric and the filling material must have passed a cigarette resistance test.

Certain cover fabrics made of natural fibres are allowed to be used in non-match resistant form. However the Regulations require that furniture with these covers must have between the cover and the filling material a fire resistant 'interliner' which itself has passed a stringent fire test. These cover materials are:

- cotton
- flax (or linen)
- viscose (or rayon)
- modal
- silk
- wool.

All new furniture[57] must carry a permanent label. It is primarily the responsibility of manufacturers to ensure that the label gives the necessary information. In the case of a settee or chair the label can usually be found on the underside of the furniture or underneath any removable seating cushions. As a minimum the label must include the following information:

- a caution – CARELESSNESS CAUSES FIRE
- a batch or identification number
- whether or not the article includes an interliner
- a summary of the aspects of the regulations with which the furniture complies.

If you are worried that any items of furniture or furnishing provided in your accommodation do not meet the required standards, you should first ask your landlord for proof that these items are sufficiently fire resistant to comply with the regulations. If your landlord cannot provide this proof, you should ask for the items to be replaced. If you prefer, you could ask your landlord to remove the items in return for a reduction in the rent.

  If your landlord fails to co-operate, you should contact either a Trading Standards

57. Except mattresses and bed-bases. The labelling requirements for these are covered by BS 7177:1989.

Officer (TSO) or an Environmental Health Officer (EHO). Although TSOs are responsible for enforcing the regulations, they have no powers to enter a private residence. For this reason, local authorities usually depend on EHOs (who do have powers of entry) to inspect furniture and furnishings. However, EHOs do not have the power to seize suspect items. As a result, some local authorities arrange joint visits.

If, having inspected the items, the TSO believes that they contravene the regulations, they have the power to seize and detain them for testing, or as evidence in a prosecution. The TSO may also request from the landlord or agent information about where the items were bought, and whether they comply, in the form of receipts and safety labels. The Regulations require the supplier to provide this information.

If it is established that the items do not comply with standards, the Trading Standards Department can prosecute the person responsible for supplying them. However, legal action is only possible within six months of the date of supply of the furniture. This means that legal action must be started:

- six months from the date that the tenant moved into the property

- six months from the date that additional or replacement items were provided

Landlords or agents found guilty of failing to comply with the regulations can be sentenced to a prison term of up to six months or a fine of up to £5,000.

In August 1997, a group of students renting a house in Oxford contacted the City Council because they were concerned about a number of problems, including the condition of the furniture supplied in the property. The HMO team liaised with the County Council's Trading Standards Officers and made a joint visit to the house. The TSOs removed two chairs, a sofa and four mattresses which failed to meet the required safety standards. The furniture had been supplied by a local letting agent, whom the landlord had employed to manage the property. A prosecution was brought by Oxford Trading Standards under the Consumer Protection Act 1987. In April 1998, Oxford Magistrates Court found the letting agent guilty of supplying furniture which did not meet fire resistance standards. The magistrate imposed fines totalling £1,625 on the letting agent and ordered her to pay £1,400 in legal costs. On imposing the penalty she said: '...if you are letting property to tenants you must have regard to their safety. The Regulations are installed for the benefit of the public and must be stringently followed.'

## Local Government Ombudsman

If your local authority fails to respond to your request to inspect your home, or lets notices served on your landlord run on for months without taking further action, then you can make a complaint to the Commission for Local Administration in England – Local Government Ombudsman. The Ombudsman investigates cases of maladministration by local authorities:

**Coventry**
Commission for Local Administration in England
The Oak, No.2, Westwood Way
Westwood Business Park, Coventry CV4 8JB
Telephone 01203 695999

**London**
Commission for Local Administration in England
21 Queen Anne's Gate, London SW1H 9BU
Telephone 020 7915 3210

**York**
Commission for Local Administration in England
Beverley House, 17 Shipton Road, York YO30 5SZ
Telephone 01904 663200

# Contact your local fire authority

If you live in a hotel or boarding house, the Environmental Health Department may refer you to the local fire authority. This is because Fire Officers (FOs) are responsible for enforcing fire safety standards in such properties. It is sometimes difficult to distinguish between a hotel, bed & breakfast hotel, hostel or boarding house. This is why it is best to contact the Environmental Health Department first.

The main piece of legislation available to FOs is the Fire Precautions Act 1971.

## Fire Precautions Act 1971

This legislation requires certain premises to have a valid fire certificate. Owners or managers can be prosecuted for the continued use of buildings without a certificate.

Section 1 of this Act allows the Government to designate the types of buildings which require a certificate. Currently, the only residential premises covered are hotels and boarding houses where board and lodging is provided for more than six people.

Under section 5 of the Act, the owner or manager of designated premises must apply to the local fire authority for a fire certificate. The applicant may also be asked to submit plans of the premises. On receipt of the application, it is the duty of the fire authority to inspect the premises to check that the fire standards are satisfactory for the use of the property stated in the application. When carrying out an inspection, FOs must be satisfied with:

- the means of escape in case of fire
- the means of ensuring that escape routes can be safely and effectively used at all times
- the means for fighting fire by people in the building, both on the escape route and elsewhere
- the means for giving warning in case of fire.

If the FO is satisfied with the fire safety standards, a fire certificate is issued. This must specify the use of the premises and the standards for which it was issued. The certificate may also impose other conditions which the FO considers appropriate in the circumstances. These can include:

- records being kept of the training of all staff in fire safety procedures

- limits to the number of people who may be in the building at any one time

- the means of escape being properly maintained and kept free of obstruction.

The certificate should be kept in the premises to which it relates. This means that if you live in a hotel or boarding house, it would be reasonable for you to ask to see the fire certificate.

If the FO is not satisfied with the standards, a notice is served on the applicant, stating that a fire certificate will not be issued unless specific works to satisfy the fire safety standards are undertaken with a certain time limit. If such works have not been carried out within the time limit then the request for a fire certificate is refused. It is possible for applicants to appeal to the court against any decisions made by the fire authority.

Continued use of a building without obtaining a fire certificate, or failure to maintain the standards or abide by the conditions imposed by the certificate, is a criminal offence. Anyone committing such an offence is liable for a fine or a prison sentence, or both.

Section 10 of the Act is not restricted to hotels and boarding houses. It applies to all residential properties in multiple occupation. It allows a FO to apply to court for a Prohibition or Restriction Order, if it is felt that the risk of fire is so serious that the use of the premises should be prohibited or restricted until steps are taken to reduce the risk to a reasonable level. As the risk must be very serious (e.g. no fire precautions whatsoever in an HMO of at least three storeys with dangerous conditions), the use of these orders for residential accommodation varies widely in different fire authorities. However, occasionally the Environmental Health Department will ask the fire authority to use this power because it is a speedier way of enforcing fire safety. The use of such orders has serious implications for occupants, who may be evicted as a result. If you are worried about losing your home for this reason, you should contact your local council's homeless persons section or a housing advice centre[58].

If, after contacting the local council or fire authority, you are still worried about the standards of fire safety in your home, it may be possible to take your own legal action against the landlord or agent.

You should always seek housing advice before taking your own legal action[59].

58. See Appendix B. 59. See Appendix B.

# Taking your own legal action

## Environmental Protection Act 1990

This Act deals with statutory nuisance. Examples of this have already been described on page 68. If you believe that your landlord is causing a statutory nuisance by allowing hazards to fire safety, and the local authority refuses to serve an abatement notice, then you may be able to take your own action against your landlord to have the nuisance removed.

Section 82 of the Act allows individuals who are 'aggrieved' by statutory nuisances to complain to the magistrates court. However, at least 21 days before you start court proceedings, you must notify your landlord in writing of your intentions. You should get advice[60] about what to put in this letter and how to apply for a hearing. A court hearing will then take place and if the court agrees that the nuisance exists, or is likely to recur, it can:

- make a nuisance order requiring the person responsible to end the nuisance within a certain time, including carrying out repairs

- impose a fine of up to £5,000 on the person responsible

- if the nuisance is so serious that it makes the property unfit for human habitation, make an order banning the use of the property until it is fit

- if the person responsible or owner of the property cannot be found, direct the local authority to take steps to end the nuisance instead.

The court can also use its powers under the Criminal Courts Act 1973 to order the person responsible to pay you compensation. If the person responsible for the nuisance fails to comply with the court order, they are guilty of a criminal offence and can be fined up to £5,000.

## Landlord and Tenant Act 1985

If you are a tenant, section 11 of this Act places an obligation on your landlord to keep in repair and proper working order:

- the structure and exterior of the premises

- installations for the supply of water, gas and electricity, and sanitation

- heating installations.

This can include items which may cause a risk to fire safety such as holes in plasterwork, ill-fitting fire doors, windows which do not open, electrical wiring, and gas or electric fires or heaters.

Case-law has established that the landlord is only obliged to carry out repairs within a reasonable time of becoming aware of the problem. This means that you should inform your landlord immediately in writing if you are worried about fire hazards which your landlord has an obligation to repair under this Act.

If your landlord fails to co-operate, you can issue proceedings in the county court. The court can:

- make an order requiring the landlord to carry out specific repairs

- award you damages for your inconvenience.

# 5 What to do if standards are not met (2)

## Advice for landlords and managers

If you have checked the standards in the accommodation you own or manage, and discovered that they fail to meet the requirements, it is advisable to seek advice before you proceed with any works.

Although the Government has issued guidance on the fire safety standards expected in certain types of property (see Chapters 2 and 3), it is the local council or fire authority which is responsible for setting and enforcing these standards locally. Therefore, it is preferable to check the local authority's current requirements before fitting expensive fire precautions. This will avoid discovering at a later date that you are required to upgrade or renew the work.

## Sources of information and advice

### Landlords' Forums and Associations
A number of local councils have now set up forums for private landlords. These meet on a regular basis to discuss the latest issues, exchange good practice ideas, keep up-to-date on current legislation and find out about local initiatives and possible sources of financial assistance. Some forums also produce a newsletter and run special events and training for private landlords.

If you attend a local forum, you will be able to seek advice and assistance on how to bring the safety standards in your property in line with the requirements. Other landlords may be able to recommend local contractors who they have found to be reliable in carrying out fire safety work.

If there is no private landlords' forum in your area, then there may be a local landlords' association, where you should be able to obtain similar information.

### Environmental Health Officers
The local authority Environmental Health Department is responsible for enforcing fire safety standards in privately rented dwellings, and particularly HMOs. Environmental Health Officers (EHOs) will be able to provide you with information on the current standards required both nationally and locally.

The best way to establish what works are required is to arrange for an EHO to meet you at the dwelling to carry out an inspection. The EHO will then be able to point out any defects which threaten fire safety and discuss what can be done to rectify them. The EHO may also be able to provide you with a schedule of works, which you can use to instruct any contractors you employ to carry out the work. EHOs are a useful source of information and practical advice.

### HMO registration schemes

Your local authority may operate an HMO Registration Scheme. Such schemes require all HMOs within a certain locality, and/or of a certain type, to be registered with the local authority. The registration requirements will include adequate fire safety standards. These schemes are usually well-publicised locally and, if you own or manage a property which falls into the catchment of the registration scheme, you may have already been contacted by your local council.

### Accreditation schemes

Some local authorities operate Accreditation schemes, Licensed to Let schemes or Codes of Standards for privately rented dwellings. These are voluntary schemes, aimed at improving standards and encouraging good management practice in privately rented dwellings. Such schemes will require that the accommodation meets fire safety standards. Landlords can benefit from membership of such schemes in a number of ways. Membership could prove an advantage in attracting tenants, and members are usually offered training, advice and information in return.

## Financial assistance

Local authorities may make grants to private landlords to assist them with the financial costs of the works required to bring a property up to standard. Grants of this sort are not as readily available now as they were in the past (when there was a mandatory entitlement to grant assistance) but it is still worth making enquiries. If your local authority is concentrating on urban renewal, or if it is keen to encourage the availability of good quality, privately rented accommodation, then there will be a budget for providing financial assistance to private landlords.

Where a local authority does provide grant assistance, the following grants may be available for fire precaution works:

- Renovation grants for fire precaution works throughout the building
- Common parts grants for fire precaution works to the common parts and facilities
- HMO grants for fire safety works to make an HMO suitable for the number of occupants.

If you are unable to finance the total cost of fire safety works yourself, then you should again contact the local authority Environmental Health Department to obtain information on the local strategy and grant availability.

## Good management practice

The fire safety standards contained in this guide are, in most cases, the minimum physical standards which should be applied. Even where these standards are met, it is equally important to ensure that your management practices take fire safety into account at all times:

## Fire safety awareness

Chapter 1 of this guide illustrates how there is much less chance of a fire occurring, and much greater chance of its effects being limited, if people are aware of fire safety. It is therefore good practice to ensure that all occupants of the dwelling are regularly reminded of how to prevent a fire from starting, and what to do if there is a fire, including the correct means of escape. This can be achieved in a number of ways.

- New residents should be advised about fire prevention; shown the means of escape; and shown how to operate fire fighting equipment when they move in.

- As well as the fire safety signs required as standard (e.g. those indicating escape routes), notices should be displayed in the entrance hall, any communal kitchens and individual dwellings, reminding occupants about fire prevention and what to do if there is a fire.

- Fire drills should be carried out on a regular basis. This will familiarise occupants with the sound of the fire alarms and escape routes.

- Any staff should have full training about what to do in case of fire.

- Residents should be made aware of the importance of reporting defects and repairs as quickly as possible. In particular, the importance of reporting repairs in the common parts (e.g. defective plasterwork in the hallway). If such defects are not directly affecting residents, they may not bother to report them, presuming they will be identified when the landlord visits the property. However, common areas are also normally the escape route and so defects should be rectified as a matter of urgency.

## Regular inspection and maintenance

Fire safety is an ongoing process. The provision of fire safety features alone will not guarantee that your property and its occupants will be safe from fire. In addition to providing standard fire safety features, it is important to regularly inspect your property and test any fire safety equipment, to ensure that everything is properly maintained and functioning as it should.

During the course of your inspections, you should check that:

- There are no potential fire hazards, particularly in the common parts and escape routes. For example, faulty electrical wiring should be rectified as a matter of urgency, and any items of rubbish or furniture left in the escape routes should be removed.

- The lighting in escape routes is working correctly. This should include replacing blown light bulbs and checking that any time-delay switches are operating correctly.

- All fire warning systems and fire fighting equipment are working correctly, by carrying out regular tests in accordance with the manufacturers' recommendations.

- Any doors used as a means of escape are closing correctly and have not been jammed open.

Do not leave your property in sub-standard condition as you have legal duties and you could be leaving yourself open to civil or criminal legal action – see Chapter 4.

# 6 What to do after a fire

## Advice for occupants and their advisers

Remember that any incident in which enough heat was generated to create smoke or fumes is considered a fire. If you have had the misfortune of experiencing a fire in your home then, no matter how minor it was, you will undoubtedly have suffered some inconvenience and anxiety. If the fire was more serious, you may have been traumatised or injured, or your belongings may have been damaged. If the fire was very serious, then your home might be so badly damaged that it is difficult or impossible to live there until it has been repaired.

There are a number of things you should do if a fire has occurred in your home.

## Record your own evidence

Even if the fire was relatively minor, you may later need to prove that it occurred. This proof may be needed to ensure fire safety standards are put in place, or to have any damage rectified. For this reason, it is always worth making a record of the sequence of events leading up to, and after, the fire. This 'diary' should include:

- the date and time that the fire occurred
- how it was caused and extinguished
- names of any witnesses
- what damage was done
- who you notified.

It may also be useful to take photographs of the scene of the fire, especially before any repairs are carried out. If you incur any expenses as a result of the fire, make a note of these and keep any receipts.

## Contact the local fire authority

If the Fire Service attended the fire, they will have a record of the source of ignition, cause and spread of the fire. They may also have noted the lack of fire precautions or other safety measures. Contact the local fire authority (the telephone number will be in the telephone book) and ask for a copy of the fire report. Again, this may be a useful source of evidence in any legal action you take. Even if you managed to extinguish the fire yourself, without having to call out the Fire Service, it might be useful to contact the fire authority afterwards if you are unsure how the fire started.

## If you cannot live in your home, contact the local council

If your home has been destroyed or seriously damaged by fire, then your local council may have a duty to assist you with finding alternative accommodation. Under the Housing Act 1996, local authorities have a legal obligation to provide you with somewhere to live if you are unintentionally homeless and in priority need. You will qualify under these categories if you have no accommodation available to occupy, or it would be unreasonable to continue living in your accommodation, as a result of a fire.

If you are homeless you should contact the Homeless Persons Section at your local council (the telephone number will be in the telephone book). They will tell you if you need to make an appointment, and give you the address. If you want to obtain housing advice about doing this, see Appendix B.

## Taking legal action

If sub-standard fire safety conditions in your home were the cause of the fire, failed to contain the fire or prevented you from quickly escaping from the fire, then you may be entitled to claim financial compensation (known as damages).

The purpose of damages is not to punish the landlord but to try, as far as money can, to return you to the same position you would have been in before the fire.

Remember, you should always seek housing advice[61] before taking your own legal action.

## Defective Premises Act 1972

Section 1 of this Act places a duty on anyone who arranges or takes on building work to provide a dwelling (including the conversion and enlargement of existing buildings) to carry out their work in a professional or workmanlike manner, with proper materials, so that the dwelling will be fit for habitation when the work is complete. This duty applies to all work started after 1 January 1974. This means that if your home was built, converted or enlarged after this date without taking fire safety into account, you can take action against your landlord or any person responsible for the work (e.g. architects, surveyors, builders).

Under Section 4 of this Act, landlords owe a duty to anyone who might be affected by defects to the premises that they are reasonably safe from injury or damage to belongings. This means that the landlord owes a duty to visitors as well as residents to ensure that any defects (including defective fire precautions or means of escape) do not lead to injury or damage from fire. Injury could include harm to a person's mental condition as the result of being traumatised by a fire or, in extreme cases, the fear of being injured in a fire.

A breach of either section of this Act will entitle you to make a claim for damages.

61. See Appendix B.

# Occupiers Liability Act 1957

Section 2 of this Act places a common-law duty on occupiers to take care that anyone who has permission to be in the property is reasonably safe. The occupier is the person in control of that part of the property. This means that landlords are considered the occupiers of the common parts (i.e. the parts that are not directly let to the residents). Common parts include hallways, stairs, landings, shared kitchens and shared bathrooms.

Therefore, if you can prove that your landlord failed to take care of such areas, and this led to you (or members of your household or visitors) or your belongings being harmed by a fire, you will be entitled to make a claim for damages.

## Common law negligence

Even in cases which are not covered by the above Acts, it is still possible for occupants who have been injured, or whose belongings have been damaged, in a fire to claim for damages. This is because, under English civil law, a person who is injured physically or materially by the negligence of another can recover compensation if a duty of care is owed, and reasonable care failed to be taken.

In order to make a successful claim for damages under this common law duty, it is necessary to prove that:

- a duty was owed to you by the landlord to take care that you were safe from fire

- the landlord neglected to take reasonable care

- you have been injured either physically or materially as a result of this negligence.

Common law is developing all the time as new cases are heard. If you feel that common law is the only way that you might be able to claim damages as the result of a fire, then it is essential that you seek legal advice[62] from someone who is aware of the legal developments in this area.

## Claiming damages

In order to claim damages, you must bring legal proceedings in the County Court. If you wish to claim damages for personal injury, these proceedings must be started within three years of the fire. In other cases, the proceedings must be started within six years. This means that you do not have to start legal action straight away or while you are still living in the property. However, it is advisable to start a damages action as soon as possible.

To start legal proceedings, a court summons must be issued. The particulars of the claim should be as detailed as possible. This is why it is essential that you seek legal advice at this stage. You may be entitled to help towards the costs of this preparatory work.

There is now no limit to the amount of damages you can be awarded by the courts and, particularly in the case of personal injury, an award for damages could total several thousand pounds.

## Improving conditions

If you are still living in the property after the fire, and there is a serious danger of another fire occurring, it is possible to apply for an interim injunction with your claim for damages. Such an application will ensure that the matter is brought before a judge within a few days. If you can then prove that you are in imminent danger as a result of your landlord's breach of duty, the court may make a mandatory order that the defects are rectified within a certain time. Again, you should not attempt to obtain an injunction before seeking legal advice[63].

Whether or not you were injured in the fire, or your property was damaged, you should ensure that steps are taken to bring the fire safety standards up to at least the minimum legal requirements. This may not involve taking any legal action yourself. The different means of enforcing standards are discussed in Chapter 4.

## If someone has been killed in the fire

In the unlikely, and tragic, event that someone has been killed in the fire, an inquest will be held to establish the cause of death. The inquest is presided over by a coroner, who is responsible for recording a verdict on how the person died. In some serious cases, there may be a jury to make this decision.

### It is essential that you seek professional advice before the inquest[64]

The landlord or manager (perhaps with the assistance of a legal representative) may try to persuade the coroner or jury that the person's death did not result from a breach of fire safety standards. It is therefore important that the inquest is presented with all the relevant evidence about why the person died. This may require the experience of a legal representative, and possibly an expert witness on fire safety standards. Unfortunately, legal aid is not available for representation at an inquest. However, the 'Advice and Assistance Scheme' will provide access to a lawyer to give advice about the inquest and may also help with some of the investigative work required.

If there is evidence that the person died because of a breach of fire safety standards, or because there was a failure by the landlord, manager or anyone else to fulfil legal duties in relation to fire safety, the coroner may record a verdict of unlawful killing, rather than accidental death. This means that the landlord (or person responsible for the breach of duty) could be open to a prosecution for manslaughter.

Inquest verdicts of unlawful killing will act as a deterrent to other landlords to ensure that fire safety standards are met. This may prevent other people from being killed in a fire. An unlawful killing verdict may also encourage the local authority to introduce greater regulation of fire safety standards in private rented dwellings in the area. For these reasons, it is important that such verdicts are well-publicised. If

---

63. See Appendix B. 64. Shelter's Campaign for Bedsit Rights can assist you in obtaining suitable advice in such circumstances. Please contact us urgently if someone you know has died as a result of a fire in a privately-rented dwelling.

Shelter's Campaign for Bedsit Rights is informed about the inquest, we can help to publicise the result.

# A Appendix A:

## What is an HMO?

Section 345 of the Housing Act 1985 defines an HMO as 'a house which is occupied by persons who do not form a single household'. The Act goes no further in its definition. Consequently defining what a household is, and who might belong to it, has been left to judges.

In 1995, the Court of Appeal decided that a group of students sharing a house did form a single household and therefore the property was not an HMO. The judgement was based on nine separate factors, most of which related to the students' lifestyle, relationship and how they occupied the property (e.g. whether they lived communally and whether they had come to the property as a single group). The case resulted in some local authorities classifying fewer shared houses as HMOs.

However, a second Court of Appeal decision in July 1999 has shown that each case must be judged individually. In this case, the judges ruled that a ten bedroom house was a house in multiple occupation (HMO) because it was shared by a group of nine individual tenants who did not form a single household. The main reasons given were that, despite a friendly and communal way of living, each occupant constituted a socio-economic unit and had come to the property on an individual basis. The ratio of bedrooms to living rooms (i.e. whether occupants were likely to spend most of their time in their individual rooms) was also taken into account.

In this case, Lord Justice Swinton Thomas stated:

*The Courts should, in my judgment, be slow to restrict the powers of local authorities to deal with the risk of fire to persons who cannot properly be categorised as being a single household.*

Having said that, as a general rule the premises listed on page 19 as HMOs for fire safety purposes can all be classified as HMOs.

65. Barnes versus Sheffield City Council, Court of Appeal, 1995. 66. Rogers versus London Borough of Islington, Court of Appeal, 1999.

# Appendix B:

## Getting housing advice

At several points in this Guide we have suggested that you should, or might want to, get housing advice, for example:

- about your legal status as a tenant or other occupier
- about using the rights available to you to take legal action
- about how to use such procedures as the courts or the ombudsman
- about your legal rights if you are threatened with homelessness

### Shelterline

Shelterline is the only free nationwide, twenty-four hour telephone housing advice line. You should phone Shelterline on 0808 800 4444 if you need housing advice. Shelterline should also be able to put you in touch with local sources of housing advice, by giving you the names, addresses, telephone numbers and opening times of local housing aid services.

### Independent housing advice services

There may be independent, voluntary housing advice agencies near where you live. Such an agency will usually be able to offer you quite detailed advice and assistance.

Shelter has a network of over 40 managed or independent housing advice centres throughout England, from which you will be able to obtain advice, assistance and, in certain circumstances, advocacy services.

### Local authority housing aid centres

Most local authorities either provide their own housing aid centre for the local community or may fund one of the independent housing advice agencies. Local authority housing aid centres may provide advice for tenants and for landlords. You can find out the address and telephone number by telephoning the town hall or civic centre.

### Citizens advice bureaux

There is a nationwide network of citizens advice bureaux, which provide advice on all problems, of which housing is only one. They may refer you for more detailed help to one of the housing advice agencies above or to a local solicitor. You should be able to find out the address and telephone number of a local citizens advice bureau through the telephone directory.

### Law centres

Law centres give free legal advice and can sometimes represent you in court. You should be able to find out whether you have a local law centre through the telephone directory.

## Solicitors

Solicitors can advise you on all aspects of the law, represent you in certain courts and, if necessary, get a barrister to represent you. It is best to approach a solicitor who specialises in housing. If you do not know of a good solicitor, contact one of the advice agencies mentioned above and ask for a recommendation.

# Glossary

Fire safety has its own jargon and technical terms. The most fundamental terms are described in this Guide. Other important ones are defined below. Sometimes terms are used loosely, even by professionals, so it is worth checking what people mean.

**Access room**
A room which must be passed through in order to reach the only escape route from an inner room.

**Accommodation stairway**
A stairway which is only used for the convenience of the occupants and is not one used for escape purposes.

**Active fire safety measures**
Active fire safety measures include alarm and detector systems, sprinklers, and other facilities to fight fire. They actively do something to fight fire as opposed to passive fire safety measures.

**AFD**
Automatic fire detection and warning system.

**Alternative escape routes**
Escape routes sufficiently separated by either direction or space, or by fire-resisting construction, to ensure that one is still available should the other be affected by fire.

**Alternative exit (from a flat or maisonette)**
One of two or more exits from within a flat or maisonette, each of which is separate from the other.

**Area of higher fire risk**
Some activities and areas present a higher fire risk than is expected in other parts of the accommodation.

Such areas may include a kitchen, a boiler room, a storeroom with combustible materials. These are called areas of higher fire risk.

**Circulation spaces**
Passages, corridors, landings, hallways, lobbies and stairways forming part of an escape route.

**Compartmentation**
The division of a building into smaller areas, with fire resisting walls, doors and floors, so that an outbreak of fire can be contained.

**Dead end**
An area from which escape is possible in one direction only, or in directions less than 45 degrees apart, which are not separated by fire resisting construction.

**Emergency lighting**
Lighting provided for use when the supply to the normal lighting fails.

**Escape lighting**
Lighting provided for use when the supply to the normal lighting fails, to ensure that the means of escape can be safely and effectively used at all material times.

**Final exit**
The termination of an escape route from a building, giving direct access to a street, passageway, walkway or open space. This exit should be sited to

ensure the rapid dispersal of persons from the vicinity of a building so that they are no longer in danger from fire and/or smoke.

### Fire resisting construction
The ability of part of the actual building structure (e.g. walls, floors, doors) to meet some or all of the standards set out in BS 476 regarding stability, integrity and insulation. Stability is the resistance of a structure to any form of collapse (e.g. sliding, overturning, deforming).

### Fire risk
A combination of the probability of fire occurring and the magnitude of the consequence of fire.

### Fire Sprinkler System
The entire means of providing sprinkler protection.

### Fire stop
A seal provided to close gaps, holes or irregularities between any part of the building or services in order to restrict the passage of fire and smoke.

### Intumescent material
A material which swells to several times its original volume when subjected to heat. Provides fire-stopping and insulating properties.

### Inner room
A room from which escape is possible only by passing through another room (the access room).

### Passive fire safety measures
Ways in which a building is structured and designed to ensure safety (e.g. fire resistance structure, restricting surface spread of flame, good planning of flats).

### Protected corridor/lobby
A corridor or lobby which is adequately protected from fire in adjoining accommodation by fire resisting construction.

### Protected route
A route having an adequate degree of protection from fire, including walls (other than any part that is an external wall of a building) partitions and floors separating the route from the remainder of the building.

### Protected stairway
A stair discharging through a final exit to a place of safety (including any exit passageway between the foot of the stair and the final exit) that is adequately enclosed with fire resisting construction.

### Responsible person
A person appointed or authorised by the property owner or person having control of the property for a particular purpose (e.g. to supervise and carry out routine checks of an AFD system).

### Separating wall
A wall separating different buildings.

### Soffit
Generally any undersurface other than a ceiling. Often used when discussing staircases to mean the area underneath all the stair treads.

### Spandrel
In fire terminology usually the vertical infill panel beneath some stairs.

### Standby supply
An electricity supply that provides power to the fire detection and alarm system when the normal supply fails.

# Index